cyclingFIT

in association with

Zest
MAGAZINE

cyclingFIT

Jamie Baird

COLLINS & BROWN

First published in the United Kingdom in 2006
Collins & Brown
The Chrysalis Building
Bramley Road
London W10 6SP

An imprint of Anova Books Company Ltd

Distributed in the United States and Canada by
Sterling Publishing Co, 387 Park Avenue South, New York, NY 10016, USA.

The National Magazine Company Ltd.
Zest is the registered trademark of The National Magazine Company Ltd

1 3 5 7 9 8 6 4 2

British Library Cataloguing-in-Publication Data:
A catalogue record for this book is available from the British Library.

ISBN 1 84340 333 1

Commissioning Editor: Victoria Alers-Hankey
Design Manager: Gemma Wilson
Editors: Emma Dickens and Jane Ellis
Senior Production Controller: Morna McPherson
Designer: Simon Daley
Models: Nick Marshallsay and Vanessa Langford
Picture credits: page 3-4 © Creasource/Corbis, page 5 © Ariel Skelley/Corbis, page 14 © David Stoecklein, page 29(t) © Michael Keller/Corbis, page 112 © Wang Leng/Getty Images
pages 7, 9-10, 11, 17-18, 20, 22, 25, 26-27, 28, 29(b), 30, 33, 34-35, 39, 44-57, 104, 111, 114-115, 117 Guy Hearn
pages 64-103 Michael Wicks
Equipment on pages 16-17, 25, 26-27, 55, 57 courtesy of Halfords, www.halfords.com. For more information call 0870 870 8810

Reproduction by Anorax UK
Printed and bound in China

Acknowledgements

A huge special thanks to Emilie Hartigan for her awesome journalistic skills, who has always been there and slaved away tirelessly in Geneva putting my garbled text into readable English. My Mum and Dad for their encouragement over the years and consistent support in all my projects and sporting life. To Ann Kibel at TFA and Victoria Alers-Hankey at Collins & Brown for all of their help. To my clients for helping me hone my skills and allowing me to be part of their lives. And lastly, to the Ganoush, one day I might get you cycling as much as me.

Contents

Introduction

I have been around bicycles all my life. Being one of three boys, bikes were some of the first presents we had. As soon as we were old enough, we were thrust on to bikes with stabilisers and off we went, darting up and down the driveway causing mayhem. I can remember how Dad held me steady as I learned to ride stabiliser-free, swerving up and down our street, trying to get my balance. The neighbourhood we lived in had loads of kids roughly the same age and of course, we all used to cycle to the park and race around the block. As you might imagine, there were plenty of crashes and accidents that involved running indoors covered in blood and pulling gravel out of wounds with tweezers.

I can remember my first-ever proper bike, a real change from the hand-me-downs that I had always had. My dad and older brother made the bike for me. They wouldn't let me see it until it was finished, and for some reason I insisted on having it spray-painted orange. That was my first bike.

From an early age I learned how to fix punctures, repair brake cables, fiddle with the gears and, of course, do wheelies. I always particularly hated repairing punctures on the back wheel because it meant taking the wheel off and getting my hands dirty on the chain.

Having a bike wasn't just about fun. As a kid, it was the key to real independence. Knowing how to cycle meant being able to get around without having to ask for a lift. We would sit for ages planning bike trips that should have lasted all day, but inevitably, once underway, only lasted a couple of hours. We frequently rode the three miles into town to go shopping or buy the latest gadget for our bikes. My favourite tool was the mileometer that attached to the front wheel, and each time the wheel went around it clocked up how far I'd gone.

As I grew up, cycling became primarily a mode of transport, as I needed the bike to get to and from school. Walking was an option; it was about three miles each way, but it took forever and getting a lift from my parents was never going to happen! The school run just didn't exist in our house. So five years was spent cycling to and from school, clocking up endless miles through rain, snow and every type of weather imaginable! Spending so much time riding also meant I had my fair share of bikes stolen over the years, so I had to become an expert on bike security.

When I moved to London my bike was the first thing that was packed in the car. My daily commute was a 25-minute ride through six miles of London streets. I couldn't live by the train or bus timetables and had to be at the gym by 6.30am. I learned how to navigate London traffic and found my years of cycling as a kid paid off.

Cycling from A to B has kept me healthy and in shape throughout my life. It is time efficient and on many a day, a quicker option than other forms of transport. When it comes to a fast, fun, easy way to get fit and save the petrol money, I reckon you can't beat a bike! It's a no-brainer really!

In this book, I will provide you with all the basic information you need to build a successful and sustainable cycling programme. We will cover everything from basic physiology and the science of fitness to bike maintenance and safety.

I have tried to create a guide that is as useful to beginners as it is to seasoned cyclists. But for all my readers, regardless of experience and expertise, there is one universal rule for success: get it done! Reading about fitness, studying the particulars of conditioning is not going to make you fit. You need to put in the energy and commitment to make real changes and see the benefits. If you are ready to buckle down and make any necessary changes in your lifestyle, then turn the page and get started.

1 Cycling & the body

You don't have to be super fit to get fit on a bike, but if you start to cycle regularly you will certainly notice a gradual improvement in your fitness levels. Your cardiovascular system will start to perform more efficiently, you will strengthen and tone your major muscle groups and you may find it easier to shed unwanted weight. On top of that, cycling is a tremendous way to beat stress, get your weekly quota of fresh air and raise your endorphin levels – all of which will boost your confidence and sense of wellbeing. Happy cycling!

Choosing fitness

People cycle for a variety of reasons. Aside from being a convenient and environmentally friendly form of transport, cycling offers all kinds of health benefits.

▶ **Cardiovascular fitness** Sustained exercise causes an increase in heart rate, leading to improved efficiency of the heart, lungs and circulatory system. Over time, consistent involvement in cardiovascular activity reduces one's risk of coronary heart disease, obesity, stroke and other illness, as well as offsetting the physical effects of ageing like decreased metabolism and muscle wasting.

▶ **Muscular fitness** Cycling action promotes the build-up of lower body muscle, while the stabilising action of the core engages the abdominal muscles. Increased muscle mass raises metabolism, improves cardiovascular efficiency and increases energy levels.

▶ **Mental and emotional fitness** Exercise raises endorphin levels leading to an increased sense of wellbeing. Getting outdoors after a long day in the office is a great way to let go of work issues – and the chemical benefits of increased fitness will bring a fresh perspective to piles of paperwork.

So why cycle for fitness?

Aside from being a fun and convenient mode of transport, cycling is a surprisingly versatile type of exercise. There are a number of ways to increase your fitness on a bike, both indoors and outdoors. This scope for variety means there is a better chance you will stick with it, finding different methods to challenge yourself.

Cycling has the added advantage that it causes less wear and tear on joints and muscles than other forms of exercise. So cycling can be prescribed to older adults and people with joint and mobility problems.

A bit about fitness

All human movement requires energy – the intensity and duration of an activity determines which method of energy production the body will use. Activities that demand sudden bursts of energy, such as cycling up a steep hill, require a large and immediate production of energy, while endurance activities, like cycling on the flat, require energy to be produced more slowly and consistently over a prolonged period of time.

Depending on the intensity and duration of an activity, as well as fitness level, your body will utilise energy from two different sources: The Aerobic System (long-term energy) and the Anaerobic System (short-term and immediate energy).

The use of oxygen by the body's cells is known as oxygen uptake or consumption. At rest, the body consumes approximately 3.5 ml of oxygen per kg bodyweight per minute (ml/kg/min). The maximum amount of oxygen a person can consume (lungs), transport (heart and arteries) and use (muscles) provides enough information to determine an individual's fitness level. The more oxygen consumed, transported and used, the higher the achievable exercise intensity and, consequently, the fitter the person. When we train, our bodies adapt in order to utilise more oxygen. Some of the adaptations made are:

▶ An increase in the number of red blood cells (they carry the oxygen to the working muscles).
▶ Increased efficiency of the lungs (more oxygen passes into the bloodstream).
▶ An increase in the number of capillaries within the muscle (which allows for better distribution of oxygen within the muscle).
▶ An increase in number and size of mitochondria within the muscle (the locations in which energy is created).

All of these changes combine to create a healthier and fitter body.

Cardiovascular function improves; circulation is more efficient; excess weight dissolves and lung capacity (pulmonary health) improves. This is why consistent participation in an exercise programme can lower one's risk of fatal health risks like stroke and coronary artery disease.

The Aerobic System – long-term energy

The Aerobic system is our most important energy system. Our bodies rely on it constantly for normal functioning in everyday life. How does it work? The aerobic system produces energy in the presence of oxygen. As the intensity of an exercise increases, the exercising muscles use increasing amounts of oxygen, causing the aerobic system to burn more fuel. Because aerobic energy production utilises carbohydrates and fats as the preferred fuel, maintaining an active aerobic system is often cited as the key element in healthy weight management.

An individual's aerobic capacity is determined by the efficiency of the cardiovascular system in carrying oxygen to the muscles. Cardiovascular fitness is measured in terms of aerobic capacity or VO2max.

To increase aerobic fitness the heart rate needs to be elevated (120+ bpm) for a period of 20–30 minutes as often as possible.

The Anaerobic System – short-term energy

The anaerobic energy system is the body's way of producing energy without having to depend on oxygen. The body switches into anaerobic mode when the intensity of exercise increases to a point where the heart and lungs can't supply enough oxygen to meet the body's energy demands. Instead, the anaerobic system uses specialised chemicals reserved in the body to provide the needed energy. These chemicals come in limited supply, meaning the body can only work anaerobically for brief periods.

When shifting to anaerobic mode, your body will make use of two different components depending on the situational needs:

▶ **Immediate energy** Provides instantaneous energy to react immediately

to a given situation, such as a short sprint, catching a bus or responding to danger. Very short duration: 1–10 seconds of energy.

▶ **Short-term energy** Responsible for providing the energy needed to make it to the top of a steep hill or sprint to the finishing line. Short duration: 60–180 seconds of energy.

Developing your cardiovascular system

To totally develop your cardiovascular system, both aerobic and anaerobic systems must be trained.

At rest, your muscles are working aerobically. As exercise intensity increases from rest to gentle cycling to hill climbing, the body's demand for oxygen also increases. At higher intensities it becomes more of a challenge for your cardiovascular system to deliver enough oxygen to the working muscles. If muscle cells are not trained to function under the additional stress of exercise, they may not be able to extract oxygen from the blood as intensity increases. Consequently, the delivery and utilisation of oxygen to the exercising muscles will be inadequate. At this point, your muscles have to shift to the anaerobic energy system to be able to continue exercising.

At any given time the energy systems, (aerobic, immediate anaerobic and short-term anaerobic) are functioning simultaneously. The intensity and the duration of the exercise and your fitness level determine what percentage of each system is being used.

Zones and overload

Aerobic Zone (AZ) Roughly 60–85 per cent of your maximum heart rate (MHR), this is the easiest zone to work in. Generally speaking, the pace you keep in your Aerobic Zone will be one you could sustain over a long period.

Lactate Threshold Zone (LTZ) At 85–90 per cent of your MHR, the Lactate Threshold is a more difficult zone to sustain. You need to acclimatise your system to working at this intensity. A good technique for building fitness at this level is to use an interval training system. Get in to this zone for 10+ minutes and do 3 repeats with at least a 10-minute recovery in between. These intense efforts will get the body used to functioning with greater amounts of lactate build-up.

Max VO2 Zone (MVZ) By far the hardest and most uncomfortable training zone at 90+ per cent of your MHR, Max VO2 puts your HR at its highest level. This requires great effort, but a few minutes once a week will pay huge dividends in the long run, especially by improving overall strength and power. Your aim when training in this zone is to get your heart working at maximum effort. As with Lactate Threshold intervals, these brief bursts of effort can be incorporated between Aerobic Zone intervals. Warm up in your Aerobic Zone for 10–20 minutes, do 3–5 repeats of 3 minutes at a hard pace, then easy cycling for 3–5 minutes to recover before you go again. Follow this with 10–20 minutes of a cool-down in your Aerobic Zone. For the cycling beginner, I advise at least 4–6 weeks of conditioning training within the Aerobic Zone to build a solid aerobic foundation before attempting to include more challenging zones into your training schedule.

Overload This principle applies to all types of training. It means exercise at a level slightly above that which can be normally carried out comfortably. But remember: overload needs to be progressive not excessive.

2 Equipment & maintenance

One of the most important decisions for any cyclist is which type of bike to purchase. Whether you are going to cycle indoors or outdoors, on roads or over rough terrain, it's crucial to choose a model that suits your needs. And once you've bought the bike, don't forget to have it adjusted properly. Before hitting the road, every wise cyclist will make sure they have a bit of essential equipment – a pump, puncture repair kit and spare chain are musts. Investing in items such as a good helmet, gloves, shoes and clothing to keep you warm and dry, will make your cycling experience all the more enjoyable

Choosing your bike

When it comes to choosing a bike, you might feel overwhelmed at first by the range of choices. It is important to consider your long-term goals and riding environment before making any purchase.

▶ Do you intend to ride indoors (stationary, spinning or turbo training) or outdoors?
▶ If outdoors, will you choose roads, trails or a combination of the two?
▶ Are you looking to compete or simply for a fun way to get fit?

Sorting out the answers to these easy questions will help to narrow your search. Once you've determined your goals and riding environment, the next step is to road test as many makes and models as possible.

Cycling inside

If you are opting for a stationary bike, test riding is still a necessary part of the process. A visit to your local dealer should help to determine which sort of indoor bike is best for you. It is also a good idea to try a variety at your local gym – just remember that an uncomfortable piece of equipment is an unused piece of equipment. The brief guidelines below will help you make an informed decision.

Indoor bikes

The granddaddy of gym equipment, indoor bikes come in two frame styles: upright and recumbent. Recumbent bikes are a good choice for the exercise novice, people with back problems and older riders. Upright cycles more closely simulate outdoor biking and can be a good way to condition for longer road rides. One of the most appealing aspects of an indoor bike is the convenience factor: you don't need to get kitted out, you can ride at any time of day in any season and safety isn't really an issue, as its hard to fall off.

Turbo trainer

An often overlooked option, the indoor trainer or turbo trainer, is a specialised device that allows you to adapt your outdoor bike for indoor riding. By elevating your back wheel, the turbo trainer makes it possible to cycle in place, and models with magnetic resistance mimic challenging road conditions for an improved workout. Some are also equipped with inbuilt computers to record your statistics – meaning you can compare your training metrics to those of an outdoor ride. On the weather question, the turbo trainer comes into its own, allowing you to work out even when it's miserable. The best thing about the turbo trainer is it allows you the flexibility of choosing to ride indoors, but as your bike is an outdoor bike, you can always hit the road when the mood strikes.

Cycling outside

If you have decided to go with an outdoor bike, there are a few different options to consider.

Mountain bikes

With their thick, deep treaded tyres and strong frames, mountain bikes are essential for enjoyable off-road riding. They also make a good city bike, handling cracks in the road and sudden kerbs with ease. In fact, city commuters shouldn't be discouraged from choosing a mountain bike just because of their urban riding environment. By replacing the treaded trail tyres with some slicker roadworthy models, any mountain bike can become a great urban cycle. However, I wouldn't recommend that commuters select a full suspension model, unless the suspension can be switched off, as these are really only suited to downhill trail riding and uneven terrain.

Road bikes

With their thin tyres and light frames, these fast bikes are a great choice for riders planning to log a lot of hours on tarmac. It's important to mention that while a mountain bike can be adapted for easy road riding, the same doesn't apply to road bikes hitting the trail. The streamlined frame of the road bike

means that thickly treaded trail tyres cannot be substituted with much success. The thinner metal frame is also more prone to bending and breaking, a problem when negotiating tough trails. But for those of you looking for a fast, road-friendly ride, you can't beat this bike.

Hybrids

A comfortable cross between road and mountain bikes, hybrids are a good choice for the casual commuter looking for a sturdy, versatile option. If you have a mindset towards competition, you should probably opt for a more specialised model.

Fitting your bike

While certain elements of the bike (both stationary and functional) can be adjusted for a more comfortable ride, there are several non-changeable aspects that need to be correctly sized before buying.

Frame size

The frame's dimensions determine the angle your body will take when you are reaching for the handlebars. A frame that is too big will cause you to overreach, straining your lower back and upper shoulders, while one that is too small will cause your body to hunch resulting in upper back and neck pain. A good diagnostic for testing a bike's frame is the straddle test. Stand over the bike and measure the distance between its top tube and your groin. A good fit will leave about 2 cm (¾ in) of space between them.

Frame size is equally important on an upright stationary bike and not every make can be properly adjusted to suit every person. If you find yourself experiencing back pain after indoor workouts, despite adjustments, the chances are you're on the wrong frame. Try opting for a different brand, or if that isn't an option, ride a recumbent.

Headset

The placement of the bike's headset is another important consideration when buying your machine. The height of the handlebars can be adjusted by moving the stem up and down. On some bikes, this is as simple as turning a lever to loosen the clamp holding the stem in place, while on others it may require an Allen key. In either case, it is a good idea to make such adjustments in the store before you buy as a way of ensuring that your bike is the right fit. If you find that the handlebars still seem too close or too far away after the stem has been adjusted, it may be that your frame is the problem and you need a different size.

Seat

Certainly one of the most obvious considerations when you are testing bikes
– a comfortable, well-sized seat means the difference between a good ride
and torture. To prevent injuries such as chafing, groin and hip pain, and
urinary discomfort, it is essential your seat be tilted correctly, adjusted for
your height and well padded. Depending on the style of bike you have
chosen, this last may be difficult to meet. If you are riding a model with a
particularly narrow, hard seat – like many road bikes – it is a good idea to
invest in a gel top or some other cushioning device. Padded bike shorts
are also a must. Have the salesperson where you purchase your bike
adjust the seat height and tilt on your bike before you buy – the top of the
saddle should be horizontal and on a slight downward angle. With an indoor
upright/recumbent cycle, while seat height is still a concern the angle is not
always adjustable.

The importance of maintenance

If your cycling preference has meant buying a bike, maintenance will certainly be a consideration. While it is good to visit a mechanic every so often for major tune-ups, much of the minor work can be done at home.

Basic maintenance at home

Here are a few ways you can ensure your bike stays in good nick.

Storage
Store your bike in a clean, dry place. If your bike is exposed to the elements it will rust and decay much more quickly. Treat your bike with care.

Cleaning your bike
It might seem obvious, but in the same way you run your car through the wash every so often, keeping your bike clean is an important part of regular maintenance. A clean, dry machine is less prone to rust, which eats away at the metal, weakening the frame. Washing your bike every two weeks – or more often for those riding off-road – will keep it working smoothly for years.

Bike lubrication
To ensure your bike continues to run smoothly, regularly lubricate your brakes, chain and front and rear derailleurs.

Investing in the right equipment

There are certain tools every outdoor cyclist needs to carry. Several bike companies have put together ready-to-go bike bags, which are a convenient, if slightly pricey, solution. But whether you decide to compile the bike bag yourself, or go with the pre-packaged version, here is a list of the essential bits and bobs:

- ▶ **Bicycle pump** Most bikes come equipped with a pump and mounted pump holder. Make sure that you have one installed if it is not already on the bike.
- ▶ **Extra chain** Especially for mountain bikers, having an extra chain in the kit can mean the difference between riding and walking home. Unfortunately, breaking a chain isn't as difficult as you might think, so cover yourself.
- ▶ **Chain repair tool** If you do need to change the chain, you're going to need a tool to remove the broken piece and reconnect the new chain.
- ▶ **Tyre levers (1)** Should you ever find yourself facing a flat, you're going to need a few of these. I recommend at least three.
- ▶ **Extra tubes** No bike kit is complete without at least one extra tube. Personally, I carry two – some days lightning can strike twice. Best to be prepared and save yourself the long walk home.
- ▶ **Puncture repair kit** An essential piece of equipment for any outdoor cyclist, puncture repair kits are available in speciality bike shops and should not be overlooked. Well-stocked with the necessary tools, most kits also contain a step-by-step guide to mending punctures, so it's good to practise before hitting the road.
- ▶ **Multi tool (2)** A compact multi tool is ideal for those emergency situations, as most bike parts can be adjusted or tightened with Allen keys.
- ▶ **Bike lights and reflective clothing** I cannot overly stress the importance of being seen at night. Fully functional and adequate lights are a must. Just remember to take your lights off when you lock up your bike. Lights that are positioned high up on the body, either attached to a

rucksack or a helmet, make you more visible to other road users. Do as much as you can to be seen at night by using reflective waistcoats, belts and ankle bands. (p 24: Investing in the right equipment, p28: More gear for the bike, p 32: Weather).

▶ **Bike locks** It is said that you should spend 10 per cent of the value of the bike on locks. There is nothing worse than having your bike or parts of your bike stolen. Make sure that you lock your bike to something solid and in well-lit, populated areas (p 24: Investing in right equipment, p 28: More gear for the bike).

▶ **Waterproof over-shoe (3)** There is nothing worse than soaking wet shoes and socks. These stretch fit over-shoes provide waterproof, windproof and breathable protection.

▶ **Mudguards** A rear mudguard is a must to keep that dirty water trail off your bum and back. Also a front guard can protect you from what is thrown up from the front tyre.

Repairs on the road – dealing with a flat tyre

You may be one of the lucky few who never has to endure this experience, but the odds are, if you ride regularly and log a fair number of miles, one of these days you're going to pop a flat. And believe me, there is nothing more frustrating than being miles from home and blowing out a tyre when you don't know how to fix it!

Here is a quick step-by-step guide to help you through the process:

► Remove the wheel with the faulty tyre. Generally, this is achieved by loosening the quick-release lever that holds the fork on to the hub **(1)**. If you have popped a back tyre, it is more tricky because you have to work around the chain and derailleur, but the same principle applies.

► Once removed, undo the valve on the tyre to let out any remaining air **(2)**, squeeze the tyre together around the rim, loosening it from the metal casing if the edge of the tyre which hooks into the rim (the 'bead') has become lodged and stuck.

► Using one of the tyre levers from your tool kit – you should carry several

– insert the lever under the bead and pry it loose **(3)**.

► Insert a second lever about two or three spokes from where you used the first **(3)**, progressively sliding the tyre off from the rim. This can be a tough action to get the hang of, but keep at it and it will work.

► Once you have removed the tyre from the rim, you can take the punctured tube out of the tyre casing **(4)**. Check inside the tyre to be certain there aren't any sharp bits floating around, which might have caused the original puncture. Have a quick look around the exposed wheel rim as well, just to cover your bases.

► Take the new tube from your tool kit and inflate it just a little, enough to give it shape, so you can slide it into the tyre casing.

► When replacing the newly tubed tyre onto the rim, it is important that you do not use tyre levers. Work from left and right on the tyre and manipulate the tyre to roll it over the rim with both thumbs.

► Once the tyre is repositioned on to the rim, you can re-inflate the tube to capacity **(5)**. Be careful not to overfill the tube as too much internal pressure makes the tyre prone to flats.

More gear for the bike – choosing the best kit

If you are riding out of doors, there is some equipment you will need, in addition to a puncture repair kit.

Water bottle

Every rider, whether biking inside or out, needs to stay hydrated. For the outdoor cyclist, different options exist – the standard water bottle (most bikes are equipped with a holder), or the hydration pack that can be worn like a rucksack, for those who don't want the fuss of reaching for the bottle every time they need a drink. Either option is a good one, the main thing is to get adequate fluid intake, particularly when riding in hot weather. For the indoor cyclist, a water bottle does the trick – you would look pretty stupid sitting on a stationary bike with a hydration pack strapped on.

Bike computer

Having a continuous monitor of mileage, caloric expenditure, heart rate, and speed or rpm, can be just the right motivator for pushing through the plateau to that next level of fitness. But just because you have chosen to do the majority of your riding outside doesn't mean that you can't benefit from this technology. Bike computers are available at your local specialist shop and can be easily installed to provide the same sort of information you get on a stationary model.

Gear for the rider

Helmet

Next to your bike, this is the most important investment you can make towards guaranteeing a safe riding experience. Accidents do happen, and considering that 85 per cent of all serious cycling injuries are head related, reliable protection is the best way to increase your chances of walking away unscathed. Make sure that your helmet choice meets your country's safety standards. Check for a verifying sticker inside the helmet, or the safety seal might be marked on the packaging. In either case, ask a salesperson at your local retailer for help to ensure you get the best fit and quality.

Shoes

Bicycle pedals come in a variety of shapes and styles, and it is important to make certain that your choice of shoe is well suited to the shape of your pedals. For most of us, trainers do the trick, fitting easily into most toe clips, though you may need to adjust the width of the strap. Serious competitive cyclists tend to opt for clipless pedals — requiring special shoes customised to snap on to the pedal face. For beginners, particularly those who are

still shaky on balance, these specialised shoes and pedals are not the right choice. Additionally, novice riders who find toe clips a challenge can choose to have them removed, riding with open-faced pedals instead. It comes down to personal preference – find the shoes that feel the best and stick with them.

Padded shorts and jersey

There's nothing worse than a sore bottom. A bad experience can put you off cycling for good. Padded shorts provide relief and can offset the discomfort that would end a training session ahead of schedule. They really are a must-have item.

Cycling jerseys are also a good piece of equipment to invest in, as they tend to be brightly coloured – a good safety measure – and made of moisture-resistant fabric to keep you cool once you break into a sweat.

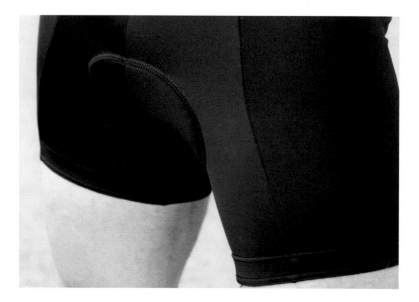

Gloves

Novice outdoor cyclists, particularly mountain bikers, are often surprised to find that some of their sorest post-ride spots are on their hands – usually it's their palms that send them screaming for the liniment. The pressure of riding uneven terrain can rub hands raw – the friction between one's grip and the vibrating handlebars makes for serious chafing. Riding gloves are an effective way to protect potentially sore palms and keep blisters at bay. And, of course, gloves keep hands warm in the winter.

Sunglasses

More than a fashion statement – sunglasses have a protective function as well. If you can't see, you're in trouble. It isn't rocket science. Sunglasses protect your eyes from insects, dust and pollutants that get kicked up by passing motorists.

Heart-rate monitor

Heart-rate monitors have become an invaluable training aid for many sports enthusiasts over the past few years. They have also become more accessible to the ordinary rider, not just the full-time sports fanatic. Using a heart-rate monitor will allow you to control the intensity of each ride – displaying your current pulse rate so you can maintain optimal training expenditure. There are a variety of models on the market at present, accommodating a range of budgets and needs. Shop around for the best fit. The straps on different brands do fit quite differently. Women often find the plastic straps uncomfortable, as they can pinch when worn with a sports bra. If you find this a problem, ask your local specialist shop about the cloth and vinyl strapped models.

Weather – gear for riding rain or shine

If you have chosen to do most of your riding out of doors, then you should be prepared to deal with all sorts of weather. The most crucial determinant of success for any fitness programme is consistency – so you need to be prepared to bike, come rain or shine. Granted, there are few things less pleasant than trying to cycle through a downpour without waterproof gear. And riding in cold temperatures without proper insulation is definitely not a pleasant experience. The only solution is to make certain you have the necessary kit to hand. And always plan ahead – pack that extra sweatshirt or pair of gloves if you expect a temperature drop. Remember, on the bike you will be exposed to wind in the best of conditions, so cooler days are going to present an extra challenge. Proper planning can mean the difference between a great ride and giving up, so make sure you are prepared.

Rain gear

It isn't the most fashionable kit, but after having been caught out a few times, you'll want to overlook that fact. A good waterproof jacket and trousers are a central part of every cyclist's wardrobe. The mistake many novices make is to only purchase the jacket – which is obviously better than nothing, but if one considers the cycling action it quickly becomes evident why the trousers are necessary. Specialist shops will have a variety of brands and styles, so you should be able to find something to suit your taste. Much of the waterproof gear is also lined for added warmth. There are also waterproof shoe covers. This is particularly important if you live in one of those places with rainy winters. You'll appreciate that extra bit of warmth, no question. Just remember – at the end of the day, it's only rain…

Winter weather gear

If you have the appropriate gear there really is no reason why winter temperatures should have to disrupt your cycling regimen. Fleece liners and lined cycling trousers, special insulating tops made with sweat-resistant material to keep you dry as your body perspires, are some of the many weather wear options to keep you comfortable in every environment. And when it comes to winter gear, don't overlook the gloves and ear warmers. These areas get particularly frozen on those long winter rides.

3 Eating & hydration

Cycling, like any form of exercise, requires good reserves of energy. Food is the body's fuel, so always aim to give your body what it needs to produce that energy. Even if you already have a healthy diet, it may be worth considering whether you could enhance your performance by making some small adjustments. Alternatively you may be trying to lose weight, so take care with your diet to ensure you have sufficient energy for cycling and still achieve weight loss. And don't forget how important it is to keep yourself properly hydrated. Giving your body the right foods and plenty of fluid will help you achieve optimal performance every time you cycle.

Food is fuel

As with any endurance activity, performance depends on the right fuel intake. Getting an appropriate nutritional balance can mean the difference between burning out on that long ride and blazing through the finish line. With so many differing theories about diet these days, it can be difficult to know what to do. The key is to keep it simple. A healthy diet incorporates protein, carbohydrate and fats in moderate amounts – you need all of these to achieve your fitness goals.

Finding the right mix

Food is the fuel that will enable you to cycle. One aspect many people overlook when planning their meals is that eating for fitness is quite different from eating for fat loss. If your training programme is specifically designed to maximise fat loss, your nutritional regime needs to complement it accordingly.

You should base your meals around slow-burning foods (see p 42: Glycemic Index) that are fibre rich, to keep you satisfied for longer, and low in sugar. Avoid heavily processed foods and simple sugar-rich carbohydrates – they are quickly metabolised and destabilise your blood sugar levels.

Protein is a vital component of any diet, but if fat loss is your aim, high-fat protein sources, such as certain cuts of meat and fried chicken, are probably best left off the menu. There has been much made in the diet industry in recent years of when to eat, and though there are a number of conflicting theories, one point holds true: if you take in fewer calories than you put out, you will lose weight. That said, there are certain timing guidelines you can follow to maximise fat loss benefits:

▶ Before a morning ride don't eat heavily. A light carbohydrate-based snack, such as a piece of fruit washed down with a glass of water, will aid effort without putting too much strain on your digestive system.

▶ If you are cycling at midday, make sure you have had a substantial breakfast and a small carbohydrate snack 1–2 hours before your workout.

▶ If you are exercising in the late afternoon or evening, then a good-sized lunch and a mid-afternoon carbohydrate-filled snack should suffice.

A bit about calories

Most of us would like to shed a few pounds and cycling can be a great way to burn off calories. However, contrary to popular belief, exercise is just one small part of the weight-loss process. Monitoring food intake is more important. Calorie counting may not be necessary, but choosing the right variety of health foods in the right amounts is imperative. Your calorie burn will vary daily, so you need to adjust your food intake to account for your activity level. Looking closely at your nutrition and making the necessary changes is the key to attaining your fitness goals.

Remember: food is fuel. When you eat, your body uses the calories from what you have consumed to provide it with energy. In order to lose weight, you need to create a calorie deficit, i.e. eat less than you burn. Men generally need to consume more calories than women, due to the amount of muscle mass a man carries. The more muscle you have, the more calories you will require to preserve that muscle.

Calories and cycling

Cycling outdoors uses more calories than cycling a similar course indoors. However, research suggests that the higher the intensity of an activity, the greater the amount of derived energy coming from carbohydrate rather than fat. This is why cycling for fat loss involves more long, moderate intensity rides while cycling for cardiovascular conditioning involves high intensity intervals and shorter rides. Ideally, a balanced training programme will combine both strategies, but for heavy, out-of-condition exercisers, it is best to focus on normalising body weight before going into intense interval work.

Metabolic rate

Each of us is physically different. Our bodies are unique in many ways – from the rate at which we process nutrients to the amount of energy we use while cycling. One way our bodies differ individually is in metabolic rate. Resting Metabolic Rate (RMR) is basically the number of calories you burn just by living 24 hours a day, 7 days a week. The higher your RMR, the more calories you will burn at rest.

Working out your RMR

To get an estimate of your own resting metabolic rate put your details through this equation.

Women 661 + (4.38 x weight in pounds) + (4.38 x height in inches) – (4.7 x age) = RMR

Men 61 + (6.24 x weight in pounds) + (12.7 x height in inches) – (6.9 x age) = RMR

Activity multiplier Now that you have an estimate of your resting metabolic rate, you can determine how many calories you need each day to meet your bodyweight goals. To calculate your daily caloric requirement, you need to add on the amount of calories you burn through exercise or the work that you do. For example, an office worker will burn less calories a day than a postman.

Multiply your RMR by one of the following:

Sedentary activity/work	x 1.15 (completely still)
Light activity/work	x 1.3 (normal everyday activity)
Moderately active/work	x 1.4 (exercise 3 times a week)
Very active/work	x 1.6 (exercise > 4 times a week)

Everyone has a friend who can eat anything without putting on weight. Likewise, we all know someone who can just look at a bag of chips and stack on 1 kg (2 lb). It all comes down to RMR – whatever your RMR is, that determines how quickly you will gain or lose weight. If you have a slow RMR it doesn't mean you can't lose weight, it just means that you have to work harder than someone with a higher RMR. Though RMR is genetic, there are things you can do to increase it.

Your RMR makes up between 60–80 per cent of your Metabolic Rate (MR). The other 20–40 per cent comes from the work you do, your lifestyle and your activity level. The more physically demanding your job and the more often you work out, the more calories you will burn on a daily basis. On the other hand, consume more calories than your MR, and you will gradually put on weight. Here are three ways to boost your RMR and MR:

▶ Increase the amount of lean tissue (muscle mass). The bigger your engine, the more calories you burn when your engine is idling. An extra pound of muscle burns an additional 50 calories per day, that's 18,000 extra calories per year.
▶ Be more active! Your metabolism is raised by exercise or general activity. You will burn significantly more calories if you maintain an active lifestyle than if you spend your days sitting in front of the TV or a behind a desk.
▶ Eat small meals often. The digestion of food accounts for 7–13 per cent of your metabolism, as eating speeds up the metabolism due to the energy needed to digest a meal.

Nutrition – the basics

It is difficult to separate the misinformation from the truth these days but the easiest way to wade through the mass of 'expert' advice is to simply learn the basic science of nutrition. Once you have the facts, you can make an informed decision about how best to eat for your goals.

Energy values of key nutrients:

Carbohydrate (1 g) = 4.5 calories

Fat (1 g) = 9 calories

Protein (1 g) = 4.5 calories

Alcohol (1 g) = 7 calories

Fat

Not all fat is bad fat. Aside from being the most concentrated form of energy, certain types of fat can help to protect us against disease. Fats can be separated into 3 groups: essential (polyunsaturates), non-essential (saturated), and trans fats. Saturated fat – from animal foods – is what we tend to think of as 'bad' fat. Once ingested, this kind of fat will either be stored by the body or used for energy. It's fine to have some saturated fat in our diets, but not too much. Essential or polyunsaturated fats, on the other hand, have an integral role in keeping us healthy. They are used by the brain and nerves to optimise function; they assist in balancing our hormone levels and enhancing our body's response to hormones. They also boost immunity, calm inflammation and even promote healthy skin. Good sources of essential fats are seeds such as flax or pumpkin seeds and fish such as mackerel, salmon and tuna.

Benefits of Healthy Fats

▶ Energy reserve (1 g of fat = 9 calories of energy)

▶ Protection of vital organs

▶ Insulation

▶ Transports the fat soluble vitamins A, D, E & K

Protein

Research has shown that protein fills you up faster than any other food. Foods high in protein also require more energy to be expended during digestion, so you end up burning more calories as you process the food. Protein is an important nutrient because it makes up part of every cell structure in the human body and is necessary for growth of new and damaged tissue. It is used as an energy back up system and unlike carbohydrates and fat, it is stored in the form of muscle and organ tissue.

Proteins are made up of 20 smaller units called amino acids of which 12 are non-essential – the body is capable of making these – and 8 essential that cannot be made by the body and can only be supplied through healthy eating. Foods that contain all 8 essential amino acids include meat, fish, eggs, milk and diary products. Other foods such as cereals, nuts, pulses and seeds also contain protein but not a full complement of amino acids.

Carbohydrates

Carbohydrates have been getting a complete hammering by the press over the past few years and as a result there is a general ignorance about them. The bottom line is that carbohydrates are the key nutritional source for athletes providing the main source of energy for muscles. Unlike other nutrients, they can be used in the absence of oxygen, making them the body's first resource when immediate fuel is required.

Carbohydrates exist in many different forms, and it is a matter of picking the healthy varieties best suited to your training needs. Generally speaking, they can be split up into starches, vegetables, fruit, and alcohol. When it comes to the starches and the spirits, obviously moderation is key, but trying to train without a balance of healthy fruit, vegetables and whole grains is simply not sustainable.

Getting the balance right

Your energy intake needs to comprise of a combination of fats, carbohydrates and proteins.

Fat 15%–25%   **Carbs** 55%–65%   **Protein** 5%–25%

Based upon your metabolic rate calculations it is possible to apply this framework to designing a daily nutritional plan that will supply you with the energy and nutrients to meet your cycling goals.

The Glycemic index

The Glycemic Index measures how quickly foods (primarily carbohydrates) raise the body's blood sugar levels. Foods that have a lower GI reading are absorbed more slowly, giving a more sustained release of energy, which, in turn, stabilises blood sugar. According to recent research low GI foods will keep you exercising for up to 20 minutes longer than faster burning, high GI foods. That said, for regular athletes, high GI foods do have their place. They can provide a boost before, during and immediately after training. Their fast-burning chemistry means that you can refuel a lot more quickly, turning a tired workout into a sweat-filled success.

High GI foods	Moderate GI foods	Low Gi Foods
White rice	Basmati rice	Apples
Brown Rice	Carrots	Grapes
Soft drinks	Spaghetti	Berries
Sweet corn	Banana	Citrus
Potatoes	Pineapple	Peaches
Cornflakes	Avocado	Plums
Baked goods (muffins, cakes)	Baked Beans	Legumes
Dried Fruit	Muesli & porridge	Broccoli
Melon/Cantaloupe	Peas	Onions
Parsnips	Whole Grain/Rye/Pitta Bread	Asparagus
	Corn	Spinach

Vitamins & Minerals

Vitamins and minerals do not provide energy; however they are needed in certain quantities for the body to produce energy and for overall good health and general wellbeing. An individual's daily requirement will differ due to age, sex, activity level and body chemistry. Vitamins are required for physiological growth and repair, and they play an integral role in exercise performance and the functioning of the immune, hormonal, digestive, circulatory and nervous systems. Minerals have a multitude of functions within the body including: controlling fluid balance in the tissues, muscle contractions, nerve function, enzyme secretions, bones and teeth and the formation of red blood cells. However, our bodies cannot manufacture vitamins and minerals independently, so they must be obtained through the foods we eat. A balanced diet rich in un-processed foods will provide you with the necessary vitamins and minerals.

The importance of variety

When you cycle, you place stress on the body and it responds by producing free radicals, toxic molecules that damage healthy cells by destabilising their normal structures. Unless dealt with, free radicals slowly destroy the body. Antioxidants are the molecules that combat free radical damage. A select group of vitamins, antioxidants like beta-carotene and Vitamin A are found in healthy foods, like fruit and vegetables, and can help your body to repair toxic breakdown. Therefore, maintaining correct nutrition during training is essential. Getting the right balance of foods will ensure you have enough antioxidants to destroy the free radicals.

Free radicals and antioxidants

Free radicals are formed by exposure to things like pollution, tobacco smoke, alcohol, insecticides, radiation, and chemicals. They can even be caused by exposure to excessive amounts of sunlight. Additionally, eating a high-fat diet or regularly engaging in strenuous exercise can cause the excessive and uncontrolled production of free radicals.

Free radicals can have devastating health effects. A high concentration of free radicals can cause the 'bad' cholesterol to stick to the walls of your arteries, increasing your risk of a stroke or heart attack. Free radicals also react with important cellular components such as DNA or the cell membrane, leading to cell malfunction and death.

Normally, our bodies are designed to handle free radicals by combating them with antioxidants derived from healthy foods, but if antioxidants are unavailable, or if the free radical production becomes excessive, damage can occur. It is particularly important to note that free radical damage accumulates with age.

But before you panic and decide to adopt radical lifestyle changes, it is good to know that there are simple, subtle ways we can reduce free radical production in our bodies. By controlling destructive behaviours we can significantly reduce their levels within our bodies. Moderate exercise and an antioxidant-rich diet are ideal ways we can help our bodies 'deactivate' free radicals before they cause harm.

Examples of antioxidants

The principal antioxidants are vitamin E, vitamin C and beta-carotene (a pre-cursor to vitamin A). Vitamin A and beta-carotene are most abundantly found in colourful fruits and vegetables such as carrots, apricots, dark green leafy vegetables, red peppers, sweet potatoes, and blue-green algae. Vitamin E is found in nuts, whole grains, vegetable oils, and to a lesser extent in fruits and vegetables. Vitamin C is found in most fruits and vegetables, especially blackcurrants, berries, broccoli, cabbage, citrus fruits, peppers, kale, kiwi fruits, papaya, spinach, tomatoes, and watercress.

Hydration and cycling

We don't drink enough water on a daily basis. Dehydration impairs physiological function, hampers performance and increases the risk of heat illness. According to a recent study, one third of British adults don't drink enough water. Rather, they tend to opt for caffeine-based drinks, which are actually counterproductive to hydration, having a diuretic effect on the body.

You may not notice how much fluid you're losing, especially when your cycling outdoors, because it evaporates off the skin in the breeze. Don't underestimate the amount of fluid you will need to replace particular in hot weather. Rates of water loss can be up to a litre per hour. Remember to keep your water bottles filled on your bike.

The sweat loss equivalent of a 2 per cent decrease in body weight increases the stress on the body resulting in impaired performance. Preventing dehydration will allow you to work for longer and harder. It really depends on the intensity and duration of your cycle. Riding hard, for 3–4 hours in hot weather conditions is going to put you most at risk. When beginning any exercise programme, it is essential to increase your hydration levels to compensate for fluid loss during exercise. Make a habit of having a glass of water prior to cycling.

Energy drinks

Losing fluid during a ride is one thing, but losing sodium (salt) is a different ball game altogether. Water is not the only thing depleted by training, especially during longer rides. As you exercise, your body tries to maintain a constant core temperature by increasing the rate at which you sweat – however the downside is you lose sodium as well as fluid. The longer you ride, the more salt you lose.

Electrolyte (salt and mineral) and energy (carbohydrate) replacement is essential and can come in the form of sports drinks. Sometimes it can be difficult to eat solid fuels while cycling.

You don't have to spend heaps of cash on the latest sports drink. A simple orange squash can do the trick and at only a fraction of the cost. Just remember to dilute it: 1 part squash to 3 parts water and/or add a little salt (1–1.5 g or 0.035–0.052 oz) to make it an electrolyte drink.

Women and cycling

Women must be aware of the additional nutritional requirements to maintain healthy reproductive function when participating in an exercise programme. One of the most important minerals in a woman's diet is calcium. Calcium is essential for maintaining healthy bones and may even prevent high blood pressure and colon cancer. Eating habits have a big impact on bone mineral density. Make sure that your intake of calcium is 1000–1500 mg per day as well as Vitamins D, A, C, B6 & K.

Any exercise activity will strengthen bones to some degree. However, in order to achieve the best results, a balanced diet is essential. A good dose of calcium can be found in dairy products, leafy greens, nuts and seafood. And be careful, as excessive alcohol and protein intake can block the absorption of calcium.

Calculate your metabolism

Using the formula given earlier in this chapter (see p 38), figure out your Resting Metabolic Rate (RMR). Factor in your activity level and any additional exercise you may be doing.

If you are finding yourself tired or even depressed, it may be that you are taking in fewer healthy calories than you need to sustain your level of activity. If the majority of your daily intake is coming from highly processed foods, sugars or other 'empty' sources, though you might be meeting the daily requirement numerically, your body is still not getting the nutrients it needs to restore its systems and recover adequately. Over time, you will be left feeling tired, cranky and weak.

If weight loss is your goal, assessing your metabolic rate and then designing a balanced meal plan to meet your weight loss goals is the key to success. Considering that half a kilo (a pound) of fat is worth approximately 3,500 calories, to lose 0.5–1 kg (1–2 lb) a week (the safest rate for ensuring long-term success) you will need to aim for a weekly deficit of 3,500 to 7,000 calories. It is very important that your daily caloric intake does not fall below your RMR, as this will actually cause your RMR to slow down, not to mention leave you hungry, weak and prone to success-sabotaging binges. It may be advisable to meet with a nutritionist before starting any modified diet, as they can advise you on the best strategies for healthy weight loss and assist you in developing a balanced eating plan.

Keep a log

In the same way that a training log can help you spot weaknesses in your exercise programme, a food diary can highlight the nutritional deficiencies or indulgences that are sabotaging your success. By tracking your intake, you can easily spot the negative patterns that are slowing your progress (like overindulging in the afternoons or eating late at night). You might find that not having adequate protein at lunch is the constant factor preceding a lacklustre evening workout – or that skipping breakfast is the common element on days when you overeat in the evenings.

4 Cycling fit

So now you're ready to go, but first it's a good idea to do some basic checks — are your handlebars and seat adjusted correctly? If you're a novice, practise building up a comfortable pedalling rhythm and get to know your gears. All cyclists should take time to prepare for the physical challenge ahead by warming up properly before a ride and including a cool-down as part of their cycling workout. Most cyclists will want to maximise their fitness levels and there's no shortage of exercises, which, when practised regularly, will improve your overall strength and flexibility, as well as building up those all-important core muscles. You may want to consider using weights to add a new dimension to your exercise routine.

Start right

You've bought the bike or joined the gym, organised your kit and you're ready to go. So where to begin? It's time to identify your fitness goals. Setting realistic goals and designing a structured plan to reach them is a good way to build consistency into your training (see also Chapter 6). Once you have identified these elements, the next step is to get on the bike and begin practising. Proper riding technique is essential for any success. It isn't realistic to sign up for a cross-country ride while you're still mastering pedalling in the park. Identifying your fitness level will keep expectations realistic and prevent over-training and burnout.

Cycling technique – a comfortable ride

A poorly adjusted bike can mean more than an uncomfortable ride.
Ill-placed handlebars, a misaligned seat, or incorrect pedal action can lead
to muscle fatigue, injury and accidents. If you have just purchased an outdoor
bike, chances are the bike shop specialist adjusted many of the variable
components for you during fitting, but if you purchased your bicycle online or
from the classifieds, you probably need to fit it yourself. The following
elements need to be properly sized.

Seat The best way to determine seat height is to sit in the saddle with your
feet on the pedals. Rotate one pedal into
the down position. Your leg should be
slightly bent at the knee when the pedal
is at its lowest point.

The seat should be tilted downwards
slightly at the front, rather than pointing up.
This will keep your groin from going numb
on longer rides. A good method to test seat
placement is the plumb line test. Sit on the
bike and rotate the pedals so both are
horizontally aligned (your feet should be at
the same height). Have a friend drop a
weighted piece of string or yardstick from
the front of your forward knee. If your seat
is correctly positioned, the weighted end
will line up with the end of your pedal's
crank arm (the bit just before the pedal
itself). Depending on where the plumb line
ends, you might need to move your seat
forward or back.

Handlebars Your handlebars are one
component of the headset – the front

portion of the bike that holds the gear shifters, brakes and hand rests. See Chapter 2 for more on adjustment of the handlebars. Too short a distance will cause pain in your upper shoulders, while too long a distance will mean sore triceps and an aching lower back. Trial and error will help you to find the best alignment. The rider should be leaning slightly forward with relaxed arms. Note: on a spinning bike both the headset and the seat can be moved horizontally and vertically for a better fit. Ask your instructor for guidance about exact positioning.

Pedalling Most experts recommend that cyclists should maintain a pedalling cadence (rhythm) somewhere between 70–90 rpm. A smooth, consistent pedalling action can be difficult to get the hang of, so here are a few tips for getting it right:

▶ The pedal goes under the ball of your foot. Many novice cyclists will place their mid-foot over the pedal, but this is wrong. Having toe clips can offset this tendency because they prevent you from pushing your foot too far forward. Pushing through the ball of your foot provides more power and reduces strain on your knees, hips and back.

▶ As you pedal, the goal is to keep the action smooth and flowing. The revolutions should not be jarring, and if you find it difficult to hit a smooth rhythm, then you might be exerting too much effort on the downward action. Try reducing your speed and concentrating on maintaining a consistent pressure through your entire revolution.

▶ Once you have the mechanics sorted, getting a rhythm is the next step. If you are riding a stationary bike, the machine's computer will help you monitor your pace, but if you are riding outside, it might not be a bad idea to invest in a bike computer (see Chapter 2). That way you can track your cadence and ensure you are in the appropriate training zone. After you have been riding for a few weeks, you will automatically drop into your rhythm and a meter won't be so necessary.

Remember

When riding indoors, make sure that you are riding in a well-ventilated area. When riding outdoors, be alert to your environment and always ride cautiously and defensively.

Knowing your gears

Learning how to work through a bike's gears is the biggest challenge for new riders. Obviously if you are riding on a stationary bike this isn't going to be an issue, but for those who have opted to hit the road, shifting can be a real frustration at the start. The best advice I can give is practise, practise, practise. Stick with it – soon enough you'll be flipping through the levels without a thought.

Some basics to remember

There are two basic shifting models common to outdoor bikes. 'Grip' or 'rapid fire' shifting is particular to most mountain bikes and many hybrids, while road and touring bikes tend to have levers. The former are a bit easier to get the hang of and allow you to keep your hands on the bars during shifting, but in both cases the basic rule is always the same: pedal through your shifting.

The gear configuration on road bikes and mountain bikes is very similar. The gearing consists of a front derailleur (located where the pedals are) and a rear derailleur (located on the back wheel). These hubs are linked to the gear levers by cables. The gear levers are located on the handlebars of mountain bikes or the down tube of road bikes.

The right gear lever controls the rear derailleur and the left gear lever controls the front derailleur. The front derailleur will consist of up to three chain rings and the rear derailleur will consist of between five and nine cogs.

1   **Highest gear (hardest to pedal):** Biggest chain ring (front derailleur) and smallest cog (rear derailleur) **(1)**.
2   **Lowest gear (easiest to pedal):** Smallest chain ring (front derailleur) and largest cog (rear derailleur) **(2)**.

A good technique for getting started is to keep the chain on the middle chain ring (front derailleur) and practise moving through the rear derailleur cogs using the right-hand lever. The pedals need to be rotating to keep the chain moving, allowing it to slide from one rear cog to another. To ensure a smooth transition, only shift one cog at a time when practising.

For the cycling novice, make sure that your gear settings allow you to keep a cadence of between 70–90 rpm. Try to choose the lowest gear where you can maintain smooth rotations and even pedal pressure. Spinning (pedalling fast) in lower gears is also easier on your joints and better for circulation and muscle development.

Quick Pointers

The higher the gear, the greater the resistance: If you are trying to build up speed, shifting into a higher gear can help.

The lower the gear, the lower the resistance: climbing hills can be made far simpler by shifting into an appropriate gear. A common mistake when learning is to begin a climb in too high a gear. If halfway up the hill you're straining to turn the pedals, you are in too high a gear.

Think Comfort Zone: a heart-pounding hill climb or finish-line sprint is great for building conditioning over time, but the majority of your ride should be within comfortable limits.

Where to ride – choosing your riding environment

As with any exercise programme, the most important element is convenience. At the end of the day, if there is too much hassle involved, your motivation will wane and you will find excuses to avoid exercise altogether. If you're not going to be consistent with an activity, it isn't the right choice for achieving your fitness goals. Here is a look at some of your cycling options:

Outdoor riding – mountain or road

So you have opted to do most of your riding outside, but what sort of riding to do? If you are lucky enough to live in a place where the terrain offers good mountain biking, then you have a real choice to make between off-road and road. In any case, the different varieties of outdoor biking have different fitness benefits. Depending on your goals and location, one type might be better suited to your situation.

Mountain biking Off-road cycling can be a real fitness challenge. Riding trails means negotiating uneven terrain where balance is harder to maintain. The upper body is an important factor – its muscle groups engage to keep your weight balanced evenly over the bike. Your core muscle systems also play an important role, contracting to maintain stability. The incorporation of these additional muscle groups results in a more comprehensive workout than many other sorts of cycling.

Additionally, mountain bikers tend to spend more time out of the saddle than road riders – and standing on pedals makes one more agile, increasing balance. Not only that, but your joints can act as shock absorbers against uneven terrain. Biking in this upright, standing position requires added effort from the gluteals, hamstrings, quadriceps and upper body, resulting in a more comprehensive, full-body workout.

Road biking Riding the road is a great way to get fit, and a convenient alternative for those without off-road options. Paved surfaces aren't exactly hard to find – getting a good workout often requires little more than stepping out of your front door. Extended hill riding on the road is a great way to increase lower body muscle mass and contribute to overall cardiovascular fitness. When it comes to planning distance rides, road cycling provides limitless options – making it a particularly good choice for those riders looking to build core strength (see p 69) and lose weight. But the best thing about road riding has to be its accessibility. For people just starting out, finding the motivation to keep with an exercise programme can be the greatest challenge. Choosing an activity that doesn't require too much preparatory fuss is key. Road biking fits the bill nicely.

Indoor riding

Nowadays, the surge in popularity of indoor cycling classes such as spinning means that even the most gym-bound exerciser can benefit from a bicycle. Riding indoors is safe and convenient. There are many models to choose from, recumbents, spinning bikes, standard upright cycles. Find the workout that is right for you and try mixing it up for increased conditioning.

Where?

Indoors (stationary/spinning)	Outdoors (mountain/road)
Weather protected	Fresh air
Convenient	Variability of terrain
No specialist gear (bike, clothing, helmet)	Increased concentration
Beginner-friendly, safe	Increased muscle recruitment
Focus on HR conditioning	Core muscle development
Build fitness levels	Transport element

Preparing your body

Cycling has a mass appeal due to its ease of execution, lack of heavy pounding on the joints and relatively simple motion. However, as with most sports, it is important to warm up, cool down and stretch as a regular part of your exercise programme.

Just jumping on to a bike, any sort of bike, and beginning an intense workout is not a smart idea. Before you hit the road, or the stationary cycle, you must take time to prepare your muscles for the challenges ahead. Warming up beforehand is the most effective way to prevent injury during activity, and proper cooling down and stretching when you've finished will keep your body healthy for years to come.

Warming up

▶ Every exercise session should start of with a gentle warm-up period during which the body can be prepared for the up-and-coming effort.

▶ Warming up increases blood flow to the working muscles. Accelerated blood flow increases muscle and core temperatures, reducing the likelihood of muscle injury.

▶ The warm-up should be gradual and of sufficient intensity to increase internal temperature without causing fatigue or the reduction of your energy stores. Typically, the warm-up should last 5–10 minutes, progressively moving you into your workout.

▶ Though you will hear differing perspectives on this, most experts agree that stopping to stretch after your warm-up is not necessary unless you feel a particular tightness that must be addressed before your workout can continue comfortably.

Cooling down

....

As with the warm-up, the cool-down is an essential part of your workout. It involves a gradual reduction in intensity until the body returns to a resting state. An adequate cool-down allows the body to return to equilibrium and prevents blood pooling in the working muscles.

It slowly decreases the heart rate, helps speed up the removal of lactic acid and lessens the potential for post-exercise muscle soreness.

A post-recovery heart rate of below 120 bpm in 3 minutes is desirable and the heart rate should be below 100 bpm within 5 minutes. A quick recovery is dependant on your own fitness and the level of intensity and duration of the workout. A longer ride will require a longer cool-down period. If your heart rate is elevated for a long time post-exertion, you should probably reduce the intensity of the workout until your base level of fitness improves.

When you finish the on-bike cool-down, take a few additional minutes to walk and stretch before ending your workout.

Recovery

....

Recovery is just as important as the training itself. The recovery time is the time when the body gets to rebuild and adapt. In fact, lactic acid removal is accelerated by active recovery. Recovery can take many forms such as eating a healthy and nutritious diet, getting good quality sleep and going on an easy recovery ride.

Flexibility training/Stretching

Why stretch?

Flexibility is one of the most overlooked aspects of sport and a lack of it is a common precursor to injury. Limited flexibility results in restricted movement and hence greater vulnerability. Flexibility training involves the stretching of muscles and tendons in order to maintain and increase suppleness. By stretching, we improve a muscle's overall range of motion, thereby allowing the corresponding joints a greater range of motion. Experience shows that flexible individuals have fewer injuries and reduced pain and soreness. In fact, tightness in muscles can cause pain throughout the body, not just in the affected areas. Additionally, lack of flexibility causes muscular imbalance that over time can cause injury.

More benefits of stretching

► Reduced muscle soreness: post-exercise stretching following a structured cool-down period is an effective way to reduce muscular soreness after exercise.
► Increased physical performance: a flexible joint has a greater range of motion.
► Improved posture: being more flexible reduces the effort needed to achieve and maintain good posture.

Factors affecting flexibility

....

► **Heat** An increase in temperature will increase the range of motion and elasticity (suppleness) of a muscle. A decrease in temperature will result in a decrease in flexibility. This is the main reason why exercise in cooler temperatures requires a longer warm-up.

► **Age** Muscle stiffness and decreasing range of joint motion is associated with advancing age. Muscles are still able to contract, but suppleness is lost. The result is stiffer, tighter muscles. Typically, as we get older activity levels decrease. By maintaining an adequate level of activity (30 minutes of cardiovascular exercise 5 times a week) and regular muscle stretching you can slow the ageing process and minimise the stiffening effect.

► **Sex** Studies show that women are generally more flexible than men. Though scientists can't pinpoint the exact reason behind this, it is sometimes attributed to the different experiences young boys and girls have in early life.

How to stretch – the guidelines

....

Make sure that your muscles are warm before beginning a stretching workout.

Although stretching as a part of your warm-up isn't necessary unless you are experiencing muscle tightness that will impair performance, stretching at the end of your workout is very important. Here are some directions to guide you through the process:

► Avoid bouncy, jerky movements that could overstretch your muscles causing injury.

► Spend more time stretching tighter muscles and you will lessen post-workout soreness.

► Make sure that the programme is balanced, meaning that you always stretch opposing muscle groups in succession – quadriceps and hamstrings, biceps and triceps.

► Breathe slowly and deeply, increasing the stretch as you breath out.

► Do not overstretch! Stretch to the point of mild discomfort, but not pain.

A note about stretching and weather

When it is cold outside you will need to warm up for longer to raise your muscular and core body temperature sufficiently. When it is warmer your body temperature is higher, so warm-ups won't take so long.

▶ Hold the stretch in a comfortable position and you should feel the tension subside as the position is held. Relax gently into the stretch, breathe out, and then slowly push the stretch a little further.

▶ Always check the alignment of your body to make sure you are not compromising other body parts: hips should be square when stretching the hamstrings; your back should not be overarched when stretching your triceps.

▶ Hold your stretches for a minimum of 30 seconds. Holding positions for longer will have additional benefits, increasing your range of motion.

Ways to keep stretching interesting

Yoga Yoga is a great way to spend 60–90 minutes working on your flexibility, be it as part of a class, one-on-one or by yourself. The practice of yoga moves the body through a range of poses that not only aim to increase flexibility, but also build muscular endurance, strength and balance.

Pilates Another great way to increase flexibility and improve core strength, pilates is a good addition to any new fitness programme.

Stretches to include in your programme

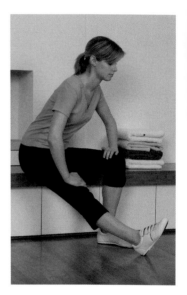

Achilles Tendon Place your right toe on to the edge of a curb or step. Bend the right knee gently forward until you feel the stretch in your right Achilles. Repeat with the other leg.

Calf Muscle Facing a wall, take your right foot directly behind you, keeping the leg straight. Bend the left knee and lean forwards into the wall. Keeping both feet pointing forwards, push the back heel into the floor and bring the hips forward. Dropping your heel off the edge of the step is another great way to stretch the calf muscle.

Hamstrings Seated Sitting on the edge of a seat, extend one leg out in front of you, keeping the knee slightly bent. Sit up tall, then bend forwards at the hips keeping your back straight. Repeat with the other leg.

 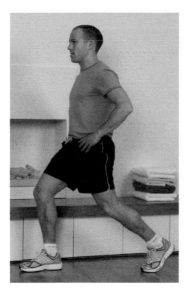 

Quadriceps Standing tall, lift one foot up behind your bum. Tuck your tail under so you feel your abdominals and glutes (bum) engage. Keep both knees together and soften the supporting knee. To increase the stretch push forward with the hip. Repeat with the other leg.

Hip Flexors Place the right foot forward and raise up on to the ball of the left foot. Tuck your tail under and push forward with your left hip. Repeat with the other leg.

Hip Flexors Kneel down and place your right foot in front of you. Gently move your bodyweight forwards (a gentle lunge), keeping both hips square so that you feel the stretch through the left hip flexor. Make sure that the right shin stays vertical above the right ankle. Repeat with the other leg.

Inner Thigh Sitting on the floor in a seated position, place the soles of your feet together out in front of you with your knees bent. Grab hold of your ankles/shins and place your elbows on the inside of your knees. Breath out and gently push down on the inside of your knees.

Glutes Lying down on your back with your knees bent. Place your left foot over your right knee. Then lift your right foot off the floor so you feel the stretch in your left glute. Repeat with the other leg.

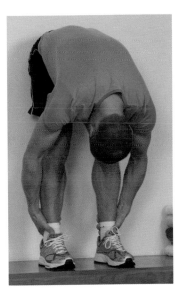  

Lower Back and Hamstrings
Standing tall with your bottom resting against the wall and knees bent slightly, bend over and take hold of the back of your calf muscles. Pull your upper body gently towards your legs. If you feel it more in the hamstrings, then bend your knees a little more.

Upper Back Standing tall, place your arms out in front of you and clasp your hands together. Turn your palms away from you and let your shoulder blades separate and relax your head.

Chest Stand in a doorframe and place one hand against the frame. Do not grip with your fingers. Gently turn your body away from the doorframe until you feel a mild stretch in the chest muscle.

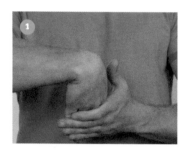

Triceps Place your left hand up in the air, bend the elbow and place your left hand between your shoulder blades. Put your right hand on top of the left elbow and apply a gentle pressure so you feel the stretch in your left tricep. Repeat on the other side.

Wrist and Forearms Place your right arm out in front of you. Place your left hand on the back of the right hand and push gently downwards.

Place your right arm out in front of you. Place your left hand on the inside of the right palm and pull your fingers towards your body.

1 Neck Place your right hand over the top of your head and gently drop the right ear down towards the right shoulder. Feel the stretch in the left side of your neck. Repeat on the other side.

2 Neck Place both hands behind your head and gently drop your chin to your chest adding a little pressure to feel the stretch in the back of the neck.

Core strength

When it comes to your body's muscular system, there are two basic types of muscle: those that stabilise (holding bones in place) and those that mobilise (move bones). Your core muscles are stabilising muscles. They keep your spine in line, thereby stabilising all the other bones in your skeleton. Exercises that focus on the lower back, glutes and abs have a great deal to offer. They help improve posture, alleviate and cure back pain, and can even help improve cycling speed. Strong abdominals are the key to good balance and control when riding a bike. Building a strong core will make it easier to maintain good cycling posture, meaning you will fatigue less quickly on those longer rides.

These days, with our increasingly sedentary lifestyles, the body's core muscles are getting less and less use. With the majority of us spending our days behind desks and our evenings on the couch, it is essential to strengthen these muscle groups through focused training. Adding abdominal and lower back exercises to your daily routine will help you build strong core muscles, preventing injury and improving performance. When the muscles of the core are weak and in a poor condition, additional stress is placed on the surrounding joint structures and muscles. In fact, a high percentage of lower back injuries and even upper and lower body injuries stem from a weakness in the core area of the body. The abdominal exercises on the following pages target a variety of muscle groups throughout your abdominal and lower back regions, and have been designed to make your overall core structure stronger.

What is the core?

Basically, your core is a network of muscles in your torso that provides you with your very own natural corset. There is so much more to abdominals than the six-pack. The deepest muscles within the abdomen are the ones that stabilise the lower back (lumbar spine). These are the transverse abdominis, pelvic floor and multifidus.

Remember

Quite frequently, core exercises are done far too quickly. Quality is over-looked for quantity. As you follow the exercises described on the follow-ing pages, focus on maintaining the form and intensity of each move-ment, rather than the number of repetitions completed.

The core provides the essential link between the upper and lower body. Think of it as the body's powerhouse. Lack of use and/or misuse will have an effect on your overall muscle function. In cycling, it is particularly important to maintain a strong torso, and not just for posture and balance. As your body's energy centre, the core provides the necessary foundations from which the legs can generate the power to push the pedals. Neglect these central muscles and you will find cycling a much greater challenge!

Exercising your core muscles

If you are thinking that lots of abdominal crunches will reduce the size of your stomach, then think again. Crunches and standard abdominal exercise only work the large muscle located beneath the fat you store around your tummy. The muscles you need to be targeting to build core strength are the more deeply set transverse abdominis and internal obliques. Just as important are the lower back and glute (butt) muscles. Along with the abdominals, they form the core and are essential for spine stabilisation. A good core workout must also incorporate the lower back muscles, the paraspinal and deep lumbar muscles.

When you walk, your body moves in a cross-pattern motion, with your opposite arm and foot simultaneously moving forward, causing your torso to rotate with each step. To work your core muscles effectively, you need to incorporate exercises that mimic this natural motion. By combining a series of rotational and cross-pattern style ab exercises, this programme will maximise impact and give you a really strong set of core muscles.

Getting started

To effectively target your core muscles, you need to work from a neutral spine position. For many, neutral spine is a very hard position to find. The back should be neither arched nor flat but somewhere in between. Before beginning any exercise, take a moment to adjust your body and make certain you are working from the correct base.

Identifying the neutral spine position

One of the best ways to find neutral is to lie on your back with your knees bent. Arch your back so you create a tunnel underneath your lower back **(1)**. Now flatten your back so that there is no tunnel and your spine is pushed firmly into the floor **(2)**. So that's an arched and a flat back. Now move from flat to arched, using your pelvis. Stop half way between the two positions so there remains a small natural arch in your lower back **(3)**. This is neutral spine and in an ideal world all exercises should be performed from this position. Keep with it and eventually you will naturally move into this position for core work.

Staying neutral

It's all well and good being able to find your neutral spine position, but the real work is being able to hold it while you perform the exercises. There are several good techniques for holding this neutral spine. Some may work better than others for you. One popular way to keep the position is by tightening your pelvic floor. Simply imagine that you are urinating and you need to stop mid-flow, or that you are dying to go to the loo but there is nowhere to go. Next, draw the belly button towards the spine without pushing the lower back into the floor. That should do the trick – or send you running to the loo …

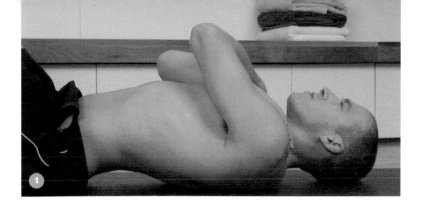

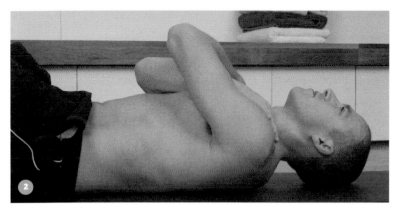

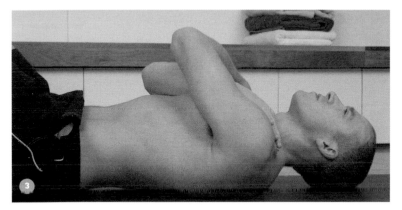

Hitting the deck

On the following pages there are several tried and tested abdominal exercises. Aim to complete between 10–20 repetitions of each exercise and 1–2 sets. Beginners should start with 1 set of 10 repetitions, building up as they get stronger.

Floor exercises

Crunch Lying on your back,
activate your pelvic floor and
draw your belly button towards
your spine without pushing your
back into the floor. Place your
hands on your temples. Slowly
lift your shoulders off the floor,
contracting your abdominals.
Hold at the top position for a
count of three and then slowly
lower back down to the floor. If
your neck hurts, then place a fist
between your chin and chest. Try
to lift with your shoulders rather
than your head.

Body Hip Lift and Bridge Lie on your back with your arms by your side and your knees bent. Tighten your abdominals and lift your hips off the floor until your body forms a straight line from your knees to your shoulders. Whilst keeping the glutes and abdominals tight, hold the position for 5–10 seconds before slowly lowering your body back down to the floor.

▶ To make the exercise harder, straighten one leg at the knee joint while maintaining a level stable pelvis.

Bicycle Crunch Lie on your back with your feet in the air. Alternately move your legs out in front of you as if you were riding a bike. As you do so touch the opposite elbow to the opposite knee. Make sure it is the outside of the elbow that touches the outside of the knee. Pause each time the knee connects with the elbow.

Plank on the Mat Kneel on the floor, lie down and position yourself on your elbows. Lift up your knees so that only your toes and forearms are in contact with the floor. Hold for 30–60 seconds. To make it harder, lift one leg 7.5 cm (3 in) off the floor, hold for a pause, return the foot and then lift the other foot.

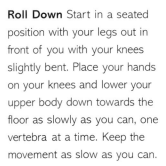

Roll Down Start in a seated position with your legs out in front of you with your knees slightly bent. Place your hands on your knees and lower your upper body down towards the floor as slowly as you can, one vertebra at a time. Keep the movement as slow as you can.

Reverse Crunch Lie on your back with knees up in the air. Then slowly using the abs pull the knees towards your head without using excessive momentum. Pull in and hold briefly and then slowly lower back to the start position.

Training on a stability ball

Stability ball training has its roots in rehabilitation: it is used by many physical therapists and orthopedic specialists worldwide. Its popularity has grown enormously within the gym and home environments in the last decade due to its versatility and simplicity. Because the ball demands balance, you will work many muscles you never knew you had, offering a fun, safe and highly effective way to exercise. As you quickly find out, you don't just get on the stability ball and begin to exercise. You can try, but you might do more harm than good. Seeking the help of a qualified trainer is always beneficial at the start.

So why use a stability ball? The use of traditional exercise equipment does not necessarily challenge whole groups of muscles in one go, and the most important muscles that act as our foundations are often overlooked. The stability ball, on the other hand, adds a new dimension to the exercise: instability. When the body is in an unstable environment, more muscles are recruited to provide the necessary stability and balance. It is the muscles of the core that stabilise the rest of the body and provide the link between the lower and upper body. Having a solid core creates a foundation upon which to perform. When used correctly, stability ball exercise calls upon constant activation of the core.

Using the stability ball and incorporating free-weight exercises is a great way to develop strength in the extremities while training the key core muscles at the same time. Even while training other muscle groups, the ab and back musculature is simultaneously working to balance and stabilise the body. Strong postural muscles and proper posture are important for relieving and preventing lower back pain. Training with the ball can improve muscle tone, increase muscular endurance and strength, restore or improve flexibility, enhance spinal stability, complement your resistance and aerobic training programmes, help you lose weight, and, lastly, improve your balance, posture and coordination.

So throw away that ab roller packed neatly underneath the bed. The stability ball is probably the best piece of training equipment you can buy.

Ball exercises

Hip Bridge on the ball (1)

Lie on your back and place both feet on top of the ball. Tighten your abdominals in the neutral position and lift your hips off the floor. Hold for 10 seconds and repeat 10 times. To make the movement harder, lift one leg off the ball when you're in the bridge position.

Hip Bridge on the ball (2)
Sit on the ball and slowly work your feet forwards and roll back down until your head and neck are resting on the ball. Drop your hips down towards the floor. Breathe out and lift your hips upwards, squeezing your glutes and abs until you reach a horizontal position. Pause for 3 seconds and then repeat.

Ball Crunch Lie down on top of the ball. Your heels should be under your knees and knees should be hip-width apart. Place your hips at a lower level than your shoulders to make the movement easier. Keep the base of your spine and the top of your bottom in contact with the ball at all times. Place your fingers next to temples, breath out and curl yourself upwards using your abs and keeping the ball motionless.

Ball Twist Crunch As above, but add a twisting motion as you curl up.

Back Extension Roll over the top of the ball keeping your toes in contact with the floor. Place your fingers next to your temples and let your upper body curve around the ball. Tighten your abs and slowly lift your upper body off the ball. Keep your eyes looking towards the floor at all times. You can do this exercise without using a ball.

Glutes Lift Roll right over the ball and rest on to your forearms on the floor. Keeping the legs together, tighten your abs and lift both your legs off the floor, squeezing your glutes and lower back. You can do this exercise without using a ball.

Forward Ball Roll Kneel behind the ball; place your hands on top of the ball. Using your knees as a pivot, keeping your core strong, slowly roll the ball forward maintaining a straight line from your shoulder to your knee. Go as far forward as you can whilst maintaining full control and a neutral spine and then pull yourself back to the start position.

Weight training

Cycling as a sport relies on the communication of several muscles at a time to achieve optimal performance. The body is designed as a link system, with all the muscles working together to function effectively. The truth is, you are really only as strong as your weakest muscle. To excel in sport, increase fitness and prevent injury, you must build a base level of strength, balancing your system. For this reason, it's important to complement any on-bike training with resistance exercises.

Weight training has become much more popular over the past decade. Gone are the days when lifting meant pumping iron in a smelly gym, surrounded by racks of huge free weights and muscle-bound bodybuilders. Instead, the proliferation of positive data about the benefits of moderate resistance training has encouraged many men and women to incorporate strength routines into their weekly regimens.

Resistance work is particularly important for those looking to lose a bit of weight and build strength. Muscle is calorie-burning material. Increasing your muscle mass will raise your basal metabolic levels, meaning you will burn more calories at rest. In fact, men and women who don't follow regular strength workouts lose about 2.3 kg (5 lb) of muscle every 10 years, lowering their metabolic rates and making weight maintenance more of a challenge.

Remember

Strength training off the bike should be done to develop strength and power, not endurance. Endurance can be built up on the bike.

Learning the Lingo

Reps Repetition of a single exercise.
Sets The number of reps of an exercise that can be performed to fatigue.
Resistance (load) The amount of weight used in an exercise
Rest The amount of time of rest in between sets.

Free weights vs. machines

Using free weights requires a greater level of skill, coordination and concentration than using a machine. Although machines have advantages over free weights – like safety and specificity – they don't teach the body to work as a link system. Instead, they tend to isolate individual muscle groups. Cables, pulleys, dumbbells and bar-bells are the best options for a variety of reasons. Wherever you go in the world, a dumbbell is still a dumbbell, and the long-term benefits of working out with free weights surpass those of machines. However, the learning curve for dumbbells and cables (free weights) is a lot greater, so patience, perseverance and proper instruction are the key.

Other benefits of weight training

- ▶ Stronger connective tissue, tendons and ligaments.
- ▶ Increased resting metabolic rate – the rate at which your body burns calories. Strength training adds muscle (or prevents loss of muscle), which has a high-energy requirement. The more muscle you have, the more energy needed for tissue maintenance and the more calories you burn.
- ▶ Greater physical capacity to perform well at your chosen sport.
- ▶ Increased bone strength and density, which is important for post-menopausal women and those prone to osteoporosis and osteoarthritis.

▶ Reduced risk of injury: your muscular system acts as the shock absorbers to prevent potential injuries from external forces and overuse.
▶ Improved injury rehabilitation: a strong, balanced muscular framework speeds recovery from injury.
▶ Core stability exercises are also essential for improving balance on the bike.

Getting started

Technique is everything when it comes to weight/strength training. Quality should be your focus, not quantity. I would much rather a client completed 10 well-executed repetitions then 15–20 poorly executed ones.

Strength training is potentially very dangerous – you can seriously injure yourself if the exercises are not performed properly. Always warm up for 5–10 minutes beforehand or do a set of light weights before you move on to the heavier, more challenging loads.

Pointers on form

Break each movement down into two parts, a lifting phase and a lowering phase. To get the most out of each lift, pause for a second in between the two phases.

Eliminate all unnecessary momentum. Any muscles not involved with the actual exercise should be holding the rest of the body still while the movement is being performed. Your bodyweight should be evenly distributed between both feet, and further evenly distributed between your heel and ball of foot. Repetitions should be slow and controlled.

Building your programme

A strength-training programme can be broken down into three distinct phases:

1 Preparation: 12–20 reps.
2 Muscle Growth: 8–12 reps.
3 Strength: 5–8 reps.

Preparation This phase introduces the body to weight training. Focus on technique and correct form. Time: 4–6 weeks. Recovery between sets: 60 seconds.

Muscle growth Aimed to increase muscle mass. Make sure muscular fatigue is hit during 8–12 reps. Make sure it's the muscle that says stop and not the brain. Time: 8–12 weeks. Recovery between sets: 60–90 seconds.

Strength This is the hardest stage due to the amount of weight you are trying to shift. Time: 4–6 weeks. Recovery between sets: 120+ seconds.

The exercises shown on the following pages aim to integrate and work a variety of muscles simultaneously. You should incorporate them into your workout routine 2 to 3 times a week.

Remember

▶ Maintain strict form: This means not swinging the weights and using lots of momentum.
▶ Lift and lower the weights in a slow and controlled manner: The muscles work and respond to weight training in both the lifting and lowering phases.
▶ Don't avoid certain exercises – always follow a balanced programme.

Strength exercises

While cycling demands an obvious effort from your legs, your upper body muscles are just as important to outdoor cycling performance (stability is not a factor on a stationary cycle). To assist in maintaining balance, the upper body works in tandem with the lower, pulling down and back on the handlebars while your legs go through the motions on the pedals. Mountain bikers will rely on these muscles even more than road cyclists, due to the ever-changing terrain and time spent out of the saddle.

All cyclists need to perform weight-training exercises to make their bodies stronger, as one only gains limited muscular strength from cycling alone. Gym-bound cyclists will need to place a special emphasis on weight training, as stationary riding doesn't require the same sort of upper body effort as outdoor biking.

Over time, as your upper body strength improves, you will find you have more energy and endurance, not to mention increased balance when riding outside. The following exercises will get you on the right track.

Upper-body exercises

Press-up Adopt a three-quarter
or full body press-up position.
Hands should be shoulder-width
and-a-half apart. Body weight
should be 70 per cent through
the hands and 30 per cent
through the feet or knees.
Keep the abdominals tight and
lower chest down to the gap
between your hands. Lower to
the point where your shoulders
are level with your elbows.
Breathe out and push yourself
back up to the starting position.

Dumbbell Chest Press

Lie, back down, on a stability ball, resting your head, neck and shoulders on the ball, while maintaining a strong horizontal body position. Hold the dumbbells above your chest. Leading with the elbows, take the dumbbells apart and lower down to a point level with your chest. Breathe out and push back up to the starting position.

 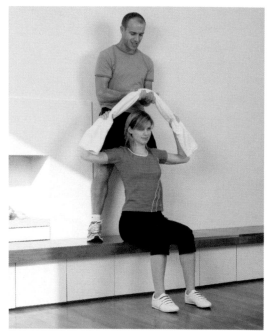

Pull-ups or Pulldowns Pull-ups can be extremely difficult to execute, because you need a lot of upper body strength to perform them. As shown above, with a partner, hold the ends of a towel above your head and pull the shoulderblades together, then pull the towel down to the top of your head leading with the elbows. As you perform the pull-down, always maintain an upright posture, with your eyes looking straight forward and a strong core. As an alternative, perform lat pull-downs on a machine.

One-arm Dumbbell Row Place your right knee and right hand lengthways on to a bench. Place your left foot out to the side. Maintain a neutral spine and tighten the abdominals. Grab a weight with the left hand and level the shoulders out. Breathe out and lift the weight up to your side, drawing the elbow close to the body. Repeat on the other side.

Reverse Flys Sit on the edge of a bench, knees together, with a couple of weights in each hand. Lean forward and rest your chest on your thighs. Keep your chest on your thighs, breathe out and retract your shoulder blades. Then lift the weights up and out to the side.

Biceps Curl and Shoulder Press Stand with
your feet hip-width apart, knees soft, tail
tucked under and abdominals engaged. Hold
a dumbbell in each hand, breathe out and lift
your arms up to your shoulders. Then turn the
dumbbells in 90 degrees and push them above
your head.

Lateral Raises Stand with your feet hip-width apart, knees soft, tail tucked under and abdominals engaged. Hold a couple of dumbbells in each hand at your sides. Breathe out and lift your arms horizontally to each side, shoulder high.

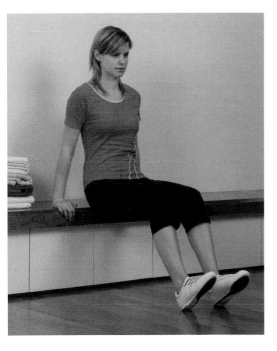 

Tricep Dips These can either be performed with
your whole bodyweight or modified to lift only a
proportion of your bodyweight. Sit on the edge of
a seat and lift your bodyweight using your arms.
Keep your feet out in front of you with your toes
elevated. Bend the elbows and lower your buttom
down towards the floor. When your elbows become
level with your shoulders, pause and return to the
starting position.

Exercises for lower body

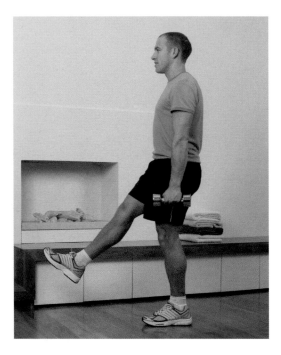 

One-legged squat Balance on your left foot. If
necessary use the back of a chair to give additional
support and balance. Place your right leg out in
front of you off the floor. Tighten the abdominals
and sit back as if you were sitting on to a chair,
while maintaining a straight back. Lower down to
the point where your thighs are almost parallel to
the floor. Repeat with the other leg.

Split Squat Take a large step out in front of you
with your right foot. Balance on the ball of the left
foot and keep the heel off the floor throughout the
entire exercise. Keeping a tall and strong upright
posture, drop the left knee down towards the floor,
making sure it doesn't touch the floor. Breathe out
and stand back up to the starting position. Repeat
with the other leg.

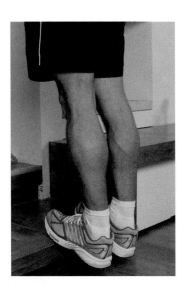
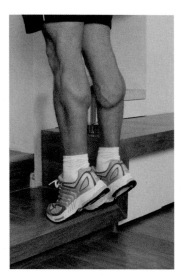

Calf Raises Stand with the balls of both feet on the edge of a step. Slowly lower your heels down towards the ground as far as they will go. Then push back up on to tiptoes while squeezing your calf muscles.

Dynamic Lunges Stand with your feet hip-width apart. Tighten your abdominals and take a large step forward with your right foot. As the right foot touches the ground, immediately drop the back left knee towards the floor, making sure that it does not hit the ground. Breathe out, re-tighten your abs, push off your front heel back to the starting position. Repeat with the other leg.

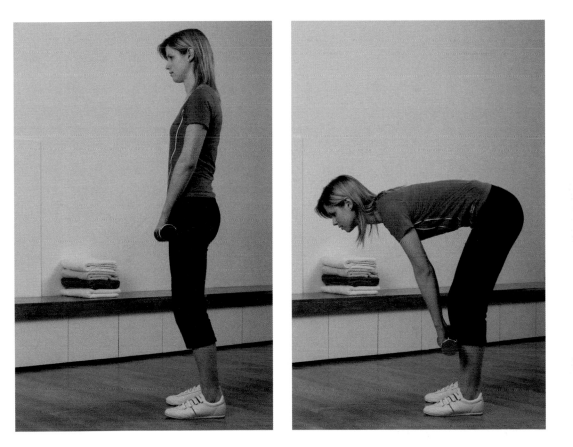

Straight-leg Dead Lift Holding a dumbbell in
each hand, stand hip-width apart, with knees
slightly bent. Slowly slide the dumbbells down the
front of your thighs to mid-shin. To do this, push
your bottom backwards without bending the knees.
When you get to the mid-shin, or feel a pulling in
the hamstrings, return to the start position by
squeezing the glutes.

Injury & safety

Every cyclist should take the basic precautions (warming up properly, wearing a helmet, maintaining their bike in good order, etc) to minimise the chances of accident and injury. Nevertheless, most cyclists will experience minor problems at some point. Common cycling injuries include saddle soreness and pain in the knees, lower back or shoulders. Identifying and treating injuries early on is vital to stop them becoming more serious – prevention is always better than cure. Familiarise yourself with the RICED system and your should be able to sort out most minor injuries, but always seek professional help if the complaint does not start to improve after a few days.

Cycling and injury

As with many sporting activities, at some point every cyclist will experience a few aches and pains. Usually all that's needed is a little rest but sometimes those aches and pains grow into more serious overuse injuries. Being able to identify and treat injuries early on is the key. By addressing our injuries when they arise, we can prevent them from getting worse and possibly from becoming chronic problems. Prevention is better than cure, so being able to nip an injury in the bud will save you a lot of heartache and discomfort in the long run.

In cycling, overuse injuries are not uncommon. Generally, affected areas are the knees, legs or back – and the culprit is usually a poorly adjusted saddle or improper pedal resistance, although there are a number of other possible causes. Upper body injuries are not as unusual in cyclists as one might assume. In fact, cycling has more upper-limb injuries than most sports. It easily beats football, basketball, running and volleyball for this dubious honour – despite the fact that most of these rely heavily on upper body action. The difference is that the cyclist is placing his/her upper body under a constant weight pressure. The task of supporting one's frame by pushing against the handlebars may seem simple, but it is actually quite taxing for the muscles involved. The most common of the resulting injuries – handlebar palsy – is a painful inflammation of the nerve running from shoulder to wrist. Handlebar palsy occurs when the arms have to absorb shock in a fixed position over a long period of time. Off-road cyclists are especially prone to this injury, given the bumpy terrain they traverse.

Most of the severe cycling injuries not tied to overuse are head related (85 per cent to be exact), and can easily be prevented by wearing a helmet. Due to the repetitive nature of cycling, where your legs power over 5,000 revolutions per hour, it's surprising that more injuries don't occur.

Why do injuries happen?

The body is a complex web of muscle, ligament, tendon and bone. To function optimally, all these elements need to be in balance. When one of these aspects is off, it throws the whole machine out of whack. Even a slight ailment, like a sore toe or strained wrist, can place undue stress on other parts. The healthy parts have to work twice as hard to compensate for weakness in the injured area, which can lead to further injury in the compensating areas. The key is to catch the original injury early on.

A checklist – the causes of injury

▶ Inadequate warm-up is a very common cause of injury. Warm muscles are more pliable and less likely to tear.

▶ Weakness or imbalance of muscle groups can be a stimulus for injury.

▶ Lapses of attention can lead to accidents. Being conscious of your environment is essential to preventing injury. Remember, everything from a light rain to a wobbly manhole cover can make the cyclist's life difficult!

▶ Neglecting your equipment, faulty brakes, loose nuts and bolts, deflated tyres, worn out cables, etc.

▶ Not wearing a helmet because it does not look trendy!

▶ Having loose clothing or items that can potentially get caught in the wheels or chain rings.

▶ Not being properly reflective at night, with reflective clothing or lights.

▶ Not adjusting your riding to suit a variety of road conditions. A slightly damp road is very greasy and can be dangerous.

▶ Not adhering to the road by-laws can be fatal, not only putting youself at risk, but other riders, drivers and pedestrians.

Common cycling injuries

Saddle soreness

Riding long distances can take a toll on your bottom, bits and bobs, making them sore and numb.

How to fix it To minimise the impact, invest in a good bike seat as well as a pair of good padded bike shorts. If chafing is a problem then use a barrier cream. Make sure you wash the affected area, dry thoroughly and apply plenty of moisturiser.

Blisters

Blisters can also manifest themselves when holding the same position on the handlebars for a prolonged period of time.

How to fix it Use gloves to alleviate blister problems.

Knee pain

Knee pain is extremely common amongst cyclists, especially those who pedal in too high (resistant) a gear. Knee pain can also occur if the saddle height is incorrectly set and if your shoe cleats are positioned incorrectly, causing discomfort and tightness.

How to fix it It's actually better to pedal in a lower (easier) gear and it's more efficient to 'spin' the pedals, meaning use a low enough gear so you can pedal with little resistance. The ideal cadence is 70–90 rpm.

NB Re-check the height of your seat every so often – perhaps once a week – because over time the seat post can slide lower, making you vulnerable to knee injury.

Arm/back pain

Maintaining a set position for long periods of time on the bike can lead to lower back, shoulder, forearm, wrist and hand ache.

How to fix it Alleviate these aches and pains by adjusting your hand position, thus taking less weight through your hands.

Lower back pain

Strain is also placed on the lower back due to poor posture and weak abdominals.

How to fix it Having a strong set of core muscles, along with an evenly balanced cycling position, will take the strain off the lower back. Weight should be evenly distributed through the handlebars and seat. The setting up of the bike is key in the long run, as it will maintain a good balance of evenly distributed weight.

Shoulder/neck pain

Shoulder ache is often due to overactive trapezius muscles and weak rhomboids (muscles between your shoulder blades). Overextension of the neck (sticking head forward) can also create tension in these areas, but particularly within the neck.

How to fix it For shoulder problems, learning to retract your shoulder blades by performing correct lateral pull downs and reverse flys will help.

To alleviate any neck pain, pull the chin into the chest as you pull the shoulder blades down and back. Stretching the neck is also an important preventative tool.

How to treat injuries

The first steps

Make a note in your training diary recording the date of onset and the pain's intensity. If you don't keep track of the injury, before long it could be a lot worse. If you haven't kept a record, you will convince yourself it's improving, when it may actually be worsening.

Next, consult a physiotherapist and listen to their advice. Too many of us assume we know the best solution for our own bodies, and attempt to fix problems beyond our capabilities. Typically injuries arise from doing too much too soon, or increasing distances, times or intensities too sharply. Respond immediately to any injury.

Self-treatment of potential injuries

If it is a simple injury, or one you have previous experience of, you may be able to forego the physio and solve the problem yourself. The basic steps are:

- Ice the injured area for 10-minute periods 3–4 times a day.
- Take an anti-inflammatory to reduce pain and inflammation.
- Cut back on your training, and if necessary, rest up for a few days.
- Stretch the area with care.
- Don't try and run through an injury, it's likely to make it a lot worse.

RICED

Every athlete is well acquainted with the RICED system for treating injury. By running through these steps consistently, you should be able to solve most minor problems. However, if after a few days the pain has not subsided or has become worse, then consult a specialist as soon as possible.

► Rest: minimize use of the injured area.

► Ice: 10–15 minutes 3–4 times a day.

► Compression: wrap the area.

► Elevation: lift the affected area above your heart while resting.

► Diagnosis: seek professional help.

Cycling safety and etiquette

Safety basics

When it comes to safety, a good rule of thumb is 'worst case scenario' visualisation. It might not sound particularly appealing, but proper consideration of all of the potential obstacles will help you to develop strategies should they arise.

In general, your level of expertise should determine the course you choose. For those starting a cycling programme, gaining or regaining confidence on a bike is the first order of business. Riding in traffic-less areas, such as parks, is a great way to build your confidence and improve quickly. Once you feel in command of the bike, you are ready to tackle the roads.

Riding outdoors and indoors

Where to ride First-time riders should stick to safe areas such as parks, trails and cycling paths. More advanced riders can opt for roads, but should try to select wide ones with good visibility.

In general, if you don't yet feel comfortable on a bike, stay out of traffic.

When to ride Generally, any time during daylight hours is a good choice. If you are riding in traffic, it might be worth taking rush hour times into account and avoiding heavily-driven thoroughfares. If you do ride in low light, at dusk or dawn, wear reflective clothing in bright colours and mount lights on your bike.

Pedestrians The number one rule to remember is: expect the unexpected. It can be difficult to judge the speed of an oncoming cyclist, and a little courtesy on the part of riders – slowing through urban areas and neighbourhoods, for instance – is much appreciated. If you plan to be riding in urban areas regularly, a bell is a necessary piece of safety equipment. That said, the courtesy equation works both ways – people are unpredictable, and cyclists tend to rank pretty low on the scale of consideration. Crossing roads and opening vehicle doors without looking are common pedestrian mistakes. The only solution is to think ahead, and remember, a bike is a vehicle and must follow the Highway Code. Pedestrians have the right of way, like it or not. Confident, defensive riding is the key.

Vehicles Cars are the main reason novice cyclists should stay off roads. Remember, just because you can see them, doesn't mean they are looking at you. When negotiating traffic, riders should stay about 0.5–1m (2–3 ft) from the side – maintaining an obvious presence in the vehicle flow. Never pass on the inside, and steer well clear of buses as they can be unpredictable. Clear signalling is also important, as is making eye contact with others on the road. A met glance reminds a driver of your presence.

Indoor safety and gym etiquette

While riding indoors poses little relative risk, there are basic etiquette guidelines to consider if riding in a public gym:

► Keeping the equipment clean – there is nothing worse than climbing on to a bike ready for your workout and finding the machine covered in sweat. Always wipe down the equipment after you finish.
► Monopolising the bike – consider those around you, particularly during peak hours. If there is a long queue for the bike, limit your riding time. A crowded gym can be a good excuse for mixing up the workout with some running or rowing. Try to schedule longer workouts outside busy times.

Tips for riding in traffic

► Ride confidently in the flow of traffic and avoid sudden swerving movement or changes of direction.
► Do not tailgate – keep a safe distance from other vehicles to allow time for necessary reactions (unexpected breaking and cars turning without signalling are common occurrences).
► Signal clearly – learn the appropriate hand signals before setting out.

Designing your programme

Now you are armed with all the basics you can design your own cycling programme. Everyone is different so it is important to tailor your programme to suit your needs. Firstly, you'll need to assess your own fitness level. Once you've established what you can do, the key is to build on this knowledge by doing the same ride time and time again. The way to achieve results is to push yourself – but be careful. It is a good idea to set yourself goals and when you achieve them you'll feel immense satisfaction. Remember to keep a log, recording all the different rides, terrains and times and before you know it you'll be registering for your first race.

Building the foundations

Building strong aerobic foundations is the key to increasing your fitness as a cyclist. Getting on the bike and going though the motions, logging those miles at a relatively good heart-rate intensity, will prove invaluable when you need to push your fitness that little bit higher.

There is a minimum amount of training time required to produce fitness improvements. The recognised training threshold for the development of cardiovascular/aerobic fitness is regarded as 20–60 minutes at an effort level of between 60–85 per cent of Maximum Heart Rate (see p 118–119 for techniques to determine your Maximum Heart Rate).

Heart rate

The easiest way to ensure the programme you are following is suited to your specific goals is to monitor your heart rate levels during exercise. Before you can design a programme to meet fitness goals, you need to customise your workouts to meet your body's needs. To calculate the different intensities best suited to your goals, you must first determine your Resting Heart Rate (RHR).

To find RHR:

The most accurate way to correctly measure your RHR is to take your pulse when you first wake up in the morning after a good night's sleep. To find your pulse, place two fingers on the side of your neck, in line with your Adam's apple, and move them until you feel the strong pulse beneath.

Heart rates

Figure out your different Heart Rate Intensities: Maximum (MHR) and Working (WHR) and Resting (RHR). There are several ways to find your maximum heart rate (MHR), some more accurate than others.

Resting Heart Rate (RHR)
Example Mr X: 60 bpm (15 beats in a 15 second interval multiplied by 4).

Maximum Heart Rate (MHR)
Method 1
For years, the formula, 220 – age, was the standard method for calculating one's maximum heart rate, but this equation has several limiting factors. The formula can be inaccurate for up to + or – 10–15 beats. That said, it does give you a useful starting point.

Method 2
A slightly more accurate, though still imperfect, equation is varied for men and women.
Men 214 – (0.8 x age)   **Women** 209 – (0.9 x age)
Despite accounting for sex, this is still a one-size-fits-all approach and quite inaccurate for a great percentage of the population.
Example Mr X: Male age 35 = 186bpm

Method 3
To find your true MHR you might want to do a stress test or VO2max (your maximum aerobic capacity) test in supervised conditions at a sports medical facility. This test, which will push your body to exhaustion, accurately measures your true MHR as well as your maximum oxygen consumption. You can be re-tested at a later date to measure improvements.

One final option, requiring your doctor's permission, is to get out on your bike with your heart rate monitor, warm up for 10–15 minutes, and then climb a steep hill as fast as you can. Record your MHR when you reach the top. This is a very effective test.

Working Heart Rate (WHR)

Subtract your Resting Heart Rate from your Maximum Heart Rate

Example Mr X: 186bpm (MHR) – 60bpm (RHR) = 126bpm (WHR)

Training zones/Exercise intensity

There are three broad training zones:

60–75% easy cycling, long slow distance

80–90% moderate to hard

90–100% hard, to really push your fitness to new levels

Find Your Training Zone in five easy steps

1. Find your Resting Heart Rate
2. Find your Maximum Heart Rate
3. Find your Working Heart Rate
4. Multiply your Working Heart Rate by your desired training zone percentage
5. Take that figure and add it to your Resting Heart Rate. The final figure is your personal target heart rate.

Training Heart Rates for Mr X

126 (WHR) x 60% = 75 + 60 (RHR) = 135 bpm

126 (WHR) x 75% = 94 + 60 (RHR) = 154 bpm

126 (WHR) x 85% = 107 + 60 (RHR) = 167 bpm

126 (WHR) x 95% = 120 + 60 (RHR) = 180 bpm

Note to Beginners

If you are new to exercise, you might find your resting heart rate on the higher than average side. As your fitness levels improve, this will adjust, so re-take your resting pulse every 2–4 weeks in order to adjust your working heart rate.

What is fitness?

The first step of any new exercise programme is gauging one's level of fitness. If you don't know where it you are starting, it's impossible to set realistic, attainable goals. But how does one determine fitness level? What does 'being fit' really mean?

Essentially, your fitness level is determined by the efficiency of your cardiovascular system. A fit system is able to deliver oxygen to working muscles effectively, reducing fatigue and promoting endurance. As fitness increases, the system delivers oxygen more successfully and performance improves. When we are unfit, the cardiovascular system is not used to functioning under stress, and consequently when we begin to exercise, our muscles don't receive the levels of oxygen efficiently enough to perform well. If the oxygen demands are greater than you can handle, then you will have to slow down or stop to catch your breath. Luckily, fitness levels adapt very quickly. What might seem impossible the first week of a new programme will be a challenge the second week, and a breeze by the third. The key is to stay consistent with your workouts so that your body adapts.

Assessing your fitness level indoors and outdoors

Here is a user-friendly yet highly individualised test you can run anytime, anywhere to help you in determining your fitness level:

▶ **Indoors** Warm up for 5–10 minutes. Select the manual programme and cycle as far as you can in 15 minutes. Record the distance and consequent heart rate along with your recovery heart rate over the next 3 minutes (recording heart rate every minute).

▶ **Outdoors** Work out a route or course from your house or place of work that will allow you to do an uninterrupted loop. Record how long it takes you to do the loop and consequent heart rate along with your recovery heart rate over the next 3 minutes (recording heart rate every minute).

It is important that you write down all the relevant information for future reference. Give yourself 6 weeks before you perform the test again and compare the results.

Training intensity – How far? How fast? How often?

The general rule of thumb with intensity and volume of training is to decrease one while increasing the other – a long steady ride or a hard shorter hill ride; or steady for 20 minutes, hard for 15 minutes, steady for 20 minutes.

To gauge how hard you're working, a simple talk test will do the trick. If you can hold a conversation, then you are in your Aerobic Zone. If you are finding it hard to string a sentence together, then you are probably in your Lactate Threshold Zone (see p 15).

Why monitor progress?

Once you got into the groove of cycling, the biggest challenge is to find new ways of building your fitness levels. Riding the same route time and time again will keep you from reaching that next level physically, not to mention boring the pants off you. There are several ways to keep one's fitness level from stagnating. The basic rule is to push your boundaries – sensibly of course, but enough that you raise the bar and force your body to adapt to new demands. Incorporating these harder sessions on a weekly basis will help you to achieve those fitness goals faster.

Ways to take your fitness to the next level

Setting SMARTER goals

SMARTER is an acronym, that is, a word made by joining the first letters of a list of other words. In this case, a SMARTER goal or objective is:

▶ **Specific** If a person sets a goal to simply 'work harder', it's too general to be of any use. It's easier to proceed with a narrower, more specific and clear goal such as, 'cycle today'.

▶ **Measurable** It's difficult to know what the scope of 'cycle today' is – the goal is still too vague. How will you know when you have achieved the goal completely? A person needs to know more about what's involved: 'Cycle today for 45 minutes'. This is one way of measuring completion. Keep in mind that a goal could have multiple measures that determine when it is complete.

▶ **Accepted, accountable** The person responsible for achieving the goal should be involved in the setting of the goal. You need to 'buy into' the goal to have a full acceptance of what it is and what will be required of you to reach it. The person who will be riding the 45 minutes should determine their route and speed. If you have built the challenge yourself, you will have a better understanding of what is involved and how likely you are to succeed.

▶ **Realistic, resources are adequate** The person or people responsible must also have the resources necessary for completion of the goal. In other words, if you determine your goal is to cycle 3 times a week for 45 minutes each time over a period of 6 months, then you probably need to have a bike…

▶ **Time frame** It must be the right time to work on the goal. There must be adequate time to complete the goal successfully with a quality effort. How the time will be organised is also important. If the goal is now 'cycle 50 miles a week', it will be useful to specify how you will break down the mileage each day, rather than leaving open the possibility that all 50 miles will be completed at the weekend. This last-minute loading is particularly bad from a fitness building perspective, as a consistent programme will have more benefit – and taxing your system heavily will lead to injury.

▶ **Extending** The goal should stretch your capabilities or make a significant contribution to the mission and purpose of your team (if you are part of a team). If there isn't a real pay-off, the goal will seem boring and without purpose, and you'll be tempted to dismiss it (so that A – acceptance and accountability – will suffer too).

▶ **Rewarding** A person should know what will result from full effort at completing the goal. It also helps to set reward benchmarks, as you near and eventually reach the goal. If your goal is to ride 3 times per week for 45 minutes, make sure you have some way of rewarding yourself for each daily ride completed on the way to the larger weekly goal. This will keep you motivated and increase your fitness levels more rapidly.

Sample SMARTER goal – competing in an event

A little light-hearted competition is a great way to get the adrenaline pumping and motivate you through those training plateaus. Knowing there is a competition around the corner might be just the thing you need to get you off the couch and into the saddle.

Training for a competition with a friend or partner is an even better way to keep spirits high, but if you're the only active one of your bunch, local bike clubs are a good place to find riding buddies.

When choosing your first competition, follow the KISS principle (Keep it Simple, Stupid), meaning don't overlook your limitations and fitness reality. If you have been riding 8 km (5 miles) a day, 4 times a week, through local parks, your first race probably shouldn't be a 50-km (30-mile) road frenzy. Your first race will be a challenge regardless of terrain or distance; just riding in a pack can be a real eye-opener. The best idea is to go with a distance you are comfortable at, and then train beyond it. Come race day, you will be more than prepared.

Planning a variety of routes with different speed/distance/terrain elements

It is important to keep your workouts interesting and challenging. By having a number of planned routes and programmes to choose from you are more likely to stick with it – always finding something to meet your fancy.

Interval training

Interval training is an effective way to build fitness once that base level of conditioning has been achieved. Basically, when you hear someone referring to 'intervals', all they really mean is an increase in intensity for a brief but sustained period. Increasing grade is also a great way to build a challenging interval workout. That said, when riding outside it can be difficult to find a series of hills suited to an interval programme. In the gym, on the other hand, it's relatively simple as most modern stationary bikes have interval programmes on their menus. One possibility for outdoor riders in flat terrain is to increase intensity using gear changes. Alternating between low and high gears on the flat is a great way to incorporate resistance intervals.

Keeping a log

Not only is this a great way to track your progress, it is a pretty strong motivator as well. Writing down your workouts means confronting just how much or how little you are doing on paper and that can be the trigger to get you in the saddle more frequently. Generally, a log should record:

► The distance
► The route or course (hill workout, speed workout, basic ride)
► Time of day
► Weather

► Total time
► Your perceived and actual exertion (use a HR monitor to determine this)

If you are particularly focused on weight loss or maintenance, you might also want to calculate the caloric expenditure of the ride so you can factor it against your daily food intake. Over time, a well-kept log becomes a sort of fitness road map, allowing you to see the holes in your training programme and design effective strategies to fill them.

Repeating rides

A great technique for determining levels of improvement, re-riding a challenging route once or twice a month will allow you to monitor how your body is adapting. If the level of difficulty doesn't seem to be decreasing, chances are you aren't challenging yourself enough on a daily basis.

Final pointers

Now that you have all the facts, get going and stick with it! Keep it interesting by:

► Joining a cycling club/group. That way you will get out for a long duration cycle with a group of fellow riders.
► Planning your routes. Sit down with a map and plan routes which take you 10, 20, 30, 40+ km (5, 10, 15, 20, 25+ miles).
► Planning routes that are predominantly flat or ones that include a variety of hills. This is not always easy – it depends where you live.
► Focussing on rotating easy, moderate and hard cycle rides. Your body needs the time to recover and replenish vital glycogen stores (carbohydrate stores). Avoid over-training.

Index